THE
ARTFUL DODGER'S
GUIDE TO PLANNING
YOUR ESTATE

3-10-98

THE
ARTFUL DODGER'S
GUIDE TO PLANNING
YOUR ESTATE

THOMAS HART HAWLEY

Illustrated by Shell Fisher

THE ONLY BOOK ON ESTATE PLANNING
GUARANTEED TO KEEP YOU ENTERTAINED

CALIFORNIA EDITION

Cover and Text Design: Irene Imfeld Graphic Design
Illustrations: Shell Fisher
Copy Editor: Diane H. Gibbs
Photographer: Steven A. Gann
Advisor: Jack Howell

Linthicum Press
P.O. Box 805
Carmel-by-the-Sea, CA 93921
Phone: (408) 624-5339
Fax: (408) 624-5839

This publication is intended to provide accurate information about se-lected estate planning topics. It is not meant to be a substitute for working di-rectly with a qualified attorney or other estate planning professional, but rather to help the reader prepare for such work.

This book is sold with the understanding that the author and the publisher are not engaged in rendering to the reader any legal, accounting, tax or other professional services.

Every attempt has been made to assure the accuracy of the material here presented, but neither the author nor the publisher assumes liability for any error or omission.

Individual copies $12.95 plus $2.00 postage and handling. Discounts avail-able for quantity orders. (See order form in back.)

Linthicum Press books are available at quantity discounts and customized editions to promote products or services. For information please write Linthicum Press, P.O. Box 805, Carmel-by-the-Sea, CA 93921.

CONTENTS

This book is dedicated to my parents,
to my own little Dodgers,
Inga and Kristina,
and to the memory of John Kaplan,
Professor of Law, Stanford University.

Acknowledgments

I want to thank the following for their criticism (constant but, usually, constructive) of the first draft of this book: Jim Cook, Esq., Marijke Hartog, Charles Hawley, Kate Hawley, Melvin Hawley, Esq., Richard Henson, Esq., Michael L. McMahan, Esq., and W.R. Rosecrans, Esq.

I am especially grateful to Doug Thompson, editor of *The Carmel Pine Cone,* for agreeing to take a chance on the column "Where There's a Will . . ." and the many Carmel subscribers (well, actually two) who urged me to write this book.

Thanks also to the long-suffering efforts of my paralegal of 25 years, Carol Jarick, for her technical assistance and advice. Thanks also to Stephanie Leach for her technical help.

And to my running buddy, Shell Fisher, whose brilliant illustrations breathe life into the characters in this book.

I did my own word processing for this book. Every few minutes or so my computer screen would flash some message like "Error message number 23 reading floppy disk drive: 1. retry 2. cancel 3. commit seppuku." Thank goodness for my friend and computer guru Howard Nieman, who never complained about the late-night calls and always had a solution.

I wish to express my gratitude to Harold Boucher for his practical suggestions and the inspiration of his excellent book, *California Living Trusts and Wills* (Pennoyer Press, 1994).

Additionally, I wish to acknowledge the truly scrutinous efforts of the copy editor, Diane H. Gibbs, and the superb cover and text design by Irene Imfeld Graphic Design.

And finally, this book would not have happened without the unflagging efforts of Jack Howell of Morning Sun Press, who shepherded the project from first draft to final publication.

Preface

During my three years in law school, I took several semesters of Taxation and Wills, Trusts and Estates. If I were not a slave to Truth, I would tell you that I coasted through these courses with much distinction. In fact, they were among the toughest courses I encountered.

Once out of law school, I was confronted with the daunting task of trying to explain to clients, usually during a single conference, estate planning concepts that had taken me months of hard work to understand. Over the years I have watched with growing concern as, five minutes into a discussion of QTIP trusts, my clients' eyes glazed over.

I went to the local bookstore for help. Unfortunately, I found that estate planning books written for the layperson offered little assistance. They fall into two categories.

There are the do-it-yourself books. These are dangerous. In any but the simplest situation, anyone preparing his or her own estate plan is likely to end up with a pig's breakfast.

There are also books that provide comprehensive explanations of our tax structure and basic planning techniques. Many of these are well written and informative. But, unfortunately, in the real world most of us are unwilling to take the time and effort to slog through these lengthy texts.

This book is my attempt to present concisely and in plain English (and, I hope, in a somewhat lighthearted fashion) the concepts you must understand to assist your attorney in developing the estate plan that is best for you.

I wish you luck in this endeavor.

Introduction

Allow me to introduce The Artful Dodger. "Art," as he is known to his friends, is undergoing a midlife crisis. At Art's age this would not be unusual except that Art's crisis is different. While most men his age suddenly go out and spend gobs of money on a red Miata convertible, Art suddenly wants to *save* gobs of money, through estate planning.

He is aided by his "clever attorney," who not only gives Art sound advice but also, on occasion, keeps him from doing something really stupid.

In these pages you will also meet Ellie Dodger, Art's wife, along with the Dodgers' son, Roger, and Roger's kids, the six little Dodgers, as well as and sundry other Dodger relations.

The villain of the piece is, of course, Uncle Sam, who doggedly tries to deprive Art of his hard-earned booty.

The Dodgers will help illustrate the ways all of us can save both income and estate taxes through basic planning techniques.

This is not a "do-it-yourself" book. Quite the contrary. Estate planning is complex and best left to the experts. Instead, this book will give you the basics you need to better assist your own clever attorney in planning your estate. By knowing something about estate planning *before* consulting your attorney, you will save yourself both time and money.

Nor is this book about exotic tax loopholes that are fabulous if they work and disastrous if they don't. The techniques discussed here are well established, and, if implemented by a professional, will not come back to disturb your sleep.

Within these pages you will not learn how to avoid paying your fair share of taxes. Rather you will learn how to minimize the impact of taxes on you and your family by making use of strategies to which Uncle Sam himself, although grudgingly, has consented.

Finally, this book is an overview. It is not intended to make a lawyer out of you. Every tax rule has an exception and every exception has a qualification and so on. These complexities may be fascinating to lawyers, but to most folks they are a bore. To encourage you to read past page 16, I have left out a lot of the tedious stuff.

One word of caution: Uncle Sam is a regular Prince Hamlet when it comes to making up his mind. One day he threatens to reduce the estate tax exemption from $600,000 to $200,000, and the next day, he promises to increase it to $1,000,000. He is always fiddling with the tax law. So be on guard for changes he may make after this book is published.

Much of the material in this book first appeared in a weekly newspaper column called "Where There's a Will . . .". For this reason, the chapters are column length, which is helpful in allowing you to traverse estate planning one short step at a time.

So come join Art and his family in what I hope will be a worthwhile and even entertaining journey to this foreign land of QTIPs, QDOTs, and QPRTs. And if you pay close attention, you might just save enough in taxes to have that red Miata convertible.

"Big book, big bore."

Callimachus
(c. 305 – c. 240 B.C.)
Hellenistic Greek poet and critic known for his brevity

THE
ARTFUL DODGER'S
GUIDE TO PLANNING
YOUR ESTATE

CHAPTER 1

Nuts and Bolts

The Artful Dodger has lately become obsessed with the idea of saving taxes. You can't blame Art. He comes by it honestly. For it was Art's grandfather Cornelius who, plagiarizing a famous Frenchman, was fond of saying, "He, who does not study taxes, is doomed to overpay them."

With the help of the Dodger clan, this little book explains in simple terms planning techniques that can save you and your family from the often devastating effect of death taxes. You cannot understand these techniques without knowing a little about our federal estate and gift tax structure. Therefore, the first two chapters will provide you with an overview of this structure.

To spare you a good deal of mind-numbing verbiage, what follows has been kept to a simple nuts-and-bolts description.

ESTATE AND GIFT TAXES: Uncle Sam taxes gifts you make during your life and at death. In medieval times (i.e., before 1977) lifetime gifts were taxed at a different rate from gifts made at death. Today the same tax rates apply to all gifts, whether they are made during life or at death.

THE $600,000 EXEMPTION: The good news is that each of you has a $600,000 exemption. This allows you to transfer either during your lifetime or at death $600,000 free of any gift or estate tax.

Let's assume, hypothetically, that Grandfather Cornelius died leaving his $1,000,000 estate to his favorite grandson, Art. (Unfortunately, this is purely hypothetical since Grandfather C. actually left all his loot to a 26-year-old aroma therapist; but that's another story.) The first $600,000 would pass free of tax. Art would pay a whopping $153,000 on the remaining $400,000, however, because the bad news is that tax rates start out high.

The first dollar over $600,000 is taxed at 37%. Rates gradually increase until they reach 55% on estates exceeding $3,000,000. Finally, in estates valued at over $10,000,000, the $600,000 exemption, like the Cheshire cat's smile, begins to disappear, until at $12,040,000, it is gone altogether.

ANNUAL EXCLUSION GIFTS: Uncle Sam also allows you to give $10,000 each year to each of any number of people tax free. This annual exclusion offers dramatic tax-saving opportunities. For example, Art has one child, Roger, and six grandchildren, the little Dodgers. Art can give $10,000 to each of these family members and instantly reduce his taxable estate by $70,000. In fact, if Art makes the gift on the evening of December 31st, he can make another gift the next morning and remove $140,000 from his estate!

Uncle Sam used to disallow any gifts made within three years of death. But no more. Now even a deathbed gift works.

THE UNLIMITED MARITAL DEDUCTION: Since 1981, transfers between spouses during lifetime or at death are not taxed. The transfers must be outright (or in other qualifying forms, which we will get into later).

In theory, Art could leave his entire estate to his wife, Ellie Dodger, who could then leave the estate to her new, presumably younger, husband, who could later leave the estate to his new, presumably younger, wife, and so on. In this way, theoretically, fortunes could pass down through the ages untaxed. In reality, most of us cannot get too excited about estate plans calculated to save taxes for our posthumous marital replacements.

Now let's take a look at how death taxes are computed. Then we will roll up our sleeves and begin looking at various ways of avoiding these taxes.

CHAPTER 2

More Nuts and Bolts

Let's see just how Uncle Sam goes about taxing your property at your death.

The Artful Dodger, when feeling expansive, often gestures towards his home, "Chez Dodger," and declares proudly to his son, Roger Dodger, "Someday, all of this will belong to you!" This is unfortunate not only because it is a cliché but also because it is not quite true. Though lacking in dramatic effect, it would be more literal to say, "Someday, all of this will belong to you . . . and your partner, Uncle Sam."

Indeed, Uncle Sam is a silent partner who lays claim to his share of your property at death. In computing that share the first step is to determine the value of your gross estate.

YOUR GROSS ESTATE: Your house, your yacht, your Nordic Track—all property you own at death is included in your gross estate. Uncle Sam, in a rare sporting gesture, allows your representative to value your property at either the date of your death or six months later.

It's a no-lose proposition since the election can be made after the six months have passed, when the values on both dates are known. For example, let's say Grandfather Cornelius's entire estate consisted of stock in Excelsior, Inc. worth $1,000,000 at his death, which declined in value to $700,000 six months later. Uncle C's executor will choose to have the estate valued six months after Uncle C's death at $700,000, thus saving tax on the $300,000 difference!

It is a common misconception that life insurance is not taxable at death. If Art owns a $100,000 policy of insurance on his life naming his son, Roger, as the beneficiary, the $100,000 will be taxable in his estate at death. If, on the other hand, Roger owns the same policy on Art's life, none of the proceeds will be taxable on Art's death and Roger will receive the $100,000 tax free.

Joint tenancy assets are included in your gross estate unless the other joint tenant contributed to the cost of the asset. For example, if Art owns a home with his son held in the name of "Art Dodger and Roger Dodger, as joint tenants," unless Roger contributed to the cost of the home, its entire value will be included in Art's estate.

The rule is different if Art holds property in joint tenancy with his wife, Ellie. Then, only half of the property is included in his gross estate regardless of who paid for the asset. The same is true of assets held with your spouse as community property.

YOUR TAXABLE ESTATE: Your taxable estate is computed by subtracting from your gross estate, certain deductions such as funeral expenses, administration expenses, and debts (your home mortgage, for example). Gifts to your spouse and to charity are also subtracted.

A "tentative" tax is then computed on your taxable estate. It is tentative because it is reduced by $192,800 (which is the tax on the $600,000 that you can transfer tax free). The effect of these machinations is to exempt from tax the first $600,000 of your taxable estate.

CALIFORNIA INHERITANCE TAX: No need to fret. There isn't any. California does impose a "pick up" tax, however. Once your estate tax is computed, a portion of it is sent to the state of California rather than to Uncle Sam. This sharing of revenue has no effect on the total estate tax. So it doesn't cost you anything.

So much for the bird's-eye view. Now let's have a look from the worm's vantage point and get on with the business of saving taxes.

CHAPTER 3

Uncle Sam's Worst Nightmare

One of the goals of the Artful Dodger, of course, is to provide for his wife, Ellie, at his death. Uncle Sam assists this goal by allowing Art to make tax-free gifts of any size to Ellie during life or at death. This is known as the "unlimited marital deduction".

Art must keep in mind one important limitation, however. The gift to Ellie must be outright—that is, without strings attached. For example, even if Art has visions of Ellie lavishing his hard-earned money on her new husband, he can't make a gift to her that will end on her remarriage.

This requirement of an outright gift once created problems for many taxpayers. For example, take the case of Art's son, Roger Dodger. Roger is married to Thelma, by whom he has six children— the little Dodgers. Thelma also has children by a prior marriage. Roger wants to leave his estate to Thelma for her use during her life. At Thelma's death, however, Roger wants what's left to pass to his kids, the six little Dodgers—not to hers.

Roger's in a bind. If he leaves his property to Thelma, outright, Thelma might just bequeath Roger's estate to her own children or, God forbid, to her new husband. If, on the other hand, Roger leaves his property to her in trust, the gift is not outright and does not qualify for the unlimited marital deduction. Consequently, at Roger's death, Thelma will pay estate tax on everything over $600,000.

THE QTIP TRUST: In an attempt to solve this problem, Uncle Sam, in 1981, created the "QTIP" trust. (Believe me, you don't want to know what QTIP stands for. But if you insist, it stands for "qualified terminal interest property.") Now Roger can leave his property to a QTIP trust for the benefit of Thelma, and have it qualify for the marital deduction. Thelma must have the right to receive all trust income. Roger also can give Thelma the right to receive support from the trust. In fact, Roger can name Thelma to act as her own trustee.

On Thelma's death, however, Roger can direct that what's left of his estate will pass to his children. The assets of the QTIP trust will be included in Thelma's estate for estate tax purposes. But any tax generated by the QTIP trust will be paid by the little Dodgers—not by Thelma's beneficiaries.

THE QDOT TRUST: After Uncle Sam gave us the unlimited marital deduction, he started having recurring nightmares. He dreamed of the millionaire who dies leaving all of his money, tax free, to his wife, who happens

to be a citizen of Raritania. The bereaved widow takes her entire inheritance back to her native Raritania. On her death it is the King of Raritania, not Uncle Sam, who collects death taxes. (At this point Uncle Sam would wake up sweaty and nearly hysterical.)

Uncle Sam created the qualified domestic trust (or "QDOT" trust) to ensure that gifts to noncitizens stayed in the United States where they eventually could be taxed. If either you or your spouse is not a U.S. citizen, you must pay close attention to what follows. Otherwise you can now skip directly to the next chapter.

Even if your spouse is not a citizen, if you leave him or her $600,000 or less, it doesn't matter, since your gift will be protected by your $600,000 exemption. If you leave your spouse more, the excess will not qualify for the marital deduction, and hence will be subject to tax, unless it passes to a QDOT trust. The most significant features of this trust are that one of the trustees must be a U.S. citizen, and estate taxes must be withheld if distributions of trust principal are made to your spouse. (Distributions of trust income, however, are not subject to estate tax.)

On your spouse's death, since the QDOT trust is in the United States rather than, for example, Raritania, Uncle Sam finally gets to collect the estate tax. As in the case of the QTIP trust, the assets of the QDOT trust are included in your spouse's taxable estate. Estate taxes generated by the assets are paid by the QDOT trust, however, not by your spouse's beneficiaries.

Did you know that many married couples waste one of their $600,000 exemptions? If you do not want the dubious distinction of being a member of this class, read on.

CHAPTER 4

Getting Two Exemptions
for the Price of One

Estate planning would be a simple matter if all the Artful Dodger had to do was write a will leaving his property to his wife, Ellie. If the gift to Ellie was outright or to a QTIP trust, Ellie would pay no estate taxes on Art's death. But Art might be creating problems down the road.

Let's assume Art leaves $1,000,000 to Ellie. At Art's death, due to the unlimited marital deduction, this gift will pass to Ellie tax free. So far so good. Now assume Ellie bequeaths $1,400,000 (consisting of the money Art left her plus $400,000 of her own money) to the Dodgers' child, Roger.

Here's the rub. The bequest to Roger is not protected by the unlimited marital deduction. It is, therefore, taxable. After deducting Ellie's $600,000 exemption, Roger will pay estate tax on the remaining $800,000 in the amount of $319,700.

Somehow Art's $600,000 exemption got lost in the shuffle. Is there any way to avoid this nasty result? Yes, and here's how.

THE BYPASS TRUST: This time let's assume that instead of leaving the entire $1,000,000 to Ellie, outright, Art places $600,000 in a bypass Trust. (It is called a bypass trust because on Ellie's death the property bypasses being taxed in her estate.) This $600,000 does not qualify for the marital deduction, but it is protected by Art's $600,000 exemption and so passes to Ellie free of tax.

Now, at Ellie's death $600,000 of her estate is not taxed because it is protected by *her* $600,000 exemption. And the $600,000 Art put in the bypass trust is not taxed either, because since Ellie didn't own it, it is not part of her estate. Roger will pay tax on only the remaining $200,000 in the amount of $74,200—a tax saving of $245,500.

Of course, Art is suspicious. "How will this bypass trust limit Ellie's enjoyment of the property?" he asks. As it turns out, not much.

Art can give Ellie one or more of these rights and still keep the property out of her estate:

(a) The right to receive all the income from the trust.
(b) The right to take from the trust whatever amounts are necessary for her reasonable support.
(c) The right to take out 5% of the value of the trust each year with no questions asked.
(d) The right to choose which children or grandchildren will inherit the property at her death.

Art can even avoid trustee's fees by naming Ellie as her own trustee. You think I'm not aware that your eyes are starting to glaze over?

This is the toughest stuff you will have to learn, so don't be discouraged. To help you through this labyrinth, I have prepared a chart (Appendix A) to show you just how all this fits together.

BALANCING THE ESTATES: When one spouse has more assets than the other spouse, it is possible to lose part of the combined $1,200,000 exemption of both spouses. Let me explain. Assume Art has separate property worth $1,200,000 and Ellie has nothing. If Art dies first, no problem (at least from the standpoint of saving taxes). Art can put $600,000 in the bypass trust and give $600,000 outright or in a QTIP trust to Ellie. At Ellie's death both the bypass trust and what's left in Ellie's estate (up to $600,000) will pass to Roger tax free.

But if Ellie dies first, since she has no assets, her $600,000 will be wasted. At Art's death, Roger will pay tax on the remaining $600,000 in Art's estate that is not protected by Art's exemption.

One solution is for Art to make a lifetime gift to Ellie of $600,000 thereby balancing both estates. Then no matter who dies first, neither spouse's exemption will be wasted.

Needless to say, prior to making any gifts to Ellie, Art should obtain independent legal advice.

OVERFUNDING THE BYPASS TRUST: Now I am going to make a really shocking suggestion. What if in our example Art put $700,000 instead of $600,000 in the bypass trust? Art's exemption protects only $600,000. True, on Art's death Ellie will pay tax on the extra $100,000. But the tax will be at the lowest estate tax rate (37%). And at Ellie's death that $100,000 (less $37,000 of estate taxes paid at Art's death) plus any appreciation will not be taxed in her estate at higher rates.

In larger estates, your spouse can actually choose to have property taxed upon your death at 37% instead of 55% at your spouse's death. In theory this is an excellent way to save taxes. In practice, however, most of us are not too keen on the idea of incurring a tax now, even at lower rates, that could be delayed until our death.

Next we'll look at an often ignored way to save your grandchildren lots of taxes.

CHAPTER 5

Passing Wealth Tax Free to Your Grandchildren

Before we go any further, I must lay to rest a persistent rumor. This book is *not* about to be made into a major motion picture starring Clint Eastwood as the unlimited marital deduction. Now that we've scotched this bit of gossip, let's get back to the business of saving taxes.

The planning techniques we've discussed so far have been aimed at saving your spouse and your children taxes. Some of you may want to take the longer view and look at ways to save your grandchildren taxes as well.

TAXING EACH GENERATION: Let's again turn to our favorite taxpayers to help illustrate. The Dodgers' son, Roger, as we know, has six children. Roger has made a fortune speculating in pork bellies. When the Dodgers leave their money to Roger, it will be taxed in the estate of either Art or Ellie—whoever dies last. Since Roger is already wealthy, he may not spend his inheritance. Therefore, at Roger's death what's left of his parents' money will be taxed again in his estate before passing to his children.

It occurs to Art, who though avaricious is not so dumb, that this double estate tax could be avoided if he gave his money directly to his grandchildren (Roger's children). In this way Art's money would not be taxed in Roger's estate but would pass directly to the little Dodgers.

For many years Art's idea worked. Taxpayers gave as much money as they wanted to their grandchildren so the money would escape being taxed in the estates of their children. Gifts of this type came to be known as generation-skipping transfers.

Uncle Sam finally said "enough is enough" and in 1976 made his first attempt to limit generation-skipping transfers.

THE $1,000,000 EXEMPTION: Today, each of us has a $1,000,000 "grandchild's exemption." This means, for example, that Art can leave $1,000,000 to his grandchildren. Just like in the good old days this

$1,000,000 will not be taxed in Roger's estate. But now Uncle Sam taxes gifts in excess of $1,000,000 to grandchildren with a vengeance. Not only will Art's estate be taxed on the amount of any gift to the little Dodgers in excess of $1,000,000, but Uncle Sam adds on a rapacious generation skipping penalty, which is due nine months after Art's death.

The trick is to limit generation-skipping transfers to $1,000,000 and not a penny more. So Art and Ellie must content themselves with giving no more than $1,000,000 each ($2,000,000 in all) to their grandchildren.

THE GENERATION-SKIPPING TRUST: Since money won speculating in pork bellies can be lost speculating in pork bellies, Ellie is worried that Roger may need the $1,000,000 after all. No problem. Instead of leaving $1,000,000 outright to her grandchildren, Ellie can leave the money, in trust, to Roger for Roger's life with the balance passing to the grandchildren at Roger's death. Roger can even be his own trustee.

If Roger needs the money, he can withdraw what he reasonably requires for his living expenses. Or Roger can leave the money in the trust and watch it grow. Of course, the income earned by the trust is taxed each year. But at Roger's death whatever is left in the trust will pass to Roger's children without being taxed in Roger's estate. If Roger has invested wisely and the $1,000,000 has increased to $4,000,000, the entire $4,000,000 will escape tax. N.G. *for kids?*

Art can do the same thing, which will pass twice as much, tax free, to the little Dodgers. In fact, Art and Ellie can first each leave the $1,000,000 to the other in trust. Only at the death of the survivor will the $2,000,000 pass into Roger's trust.

To illustrate this technique (and because I have recently become quite good at making boxes and lines on my word processor), I have prepared a chart for you (Appendix B).

BALANCING THE ESTATES: Remember in chapter 4 how a gift from Art to Ellie avoided wasting Ellie's $600,000 exemption? Good! Because the same technique applies to generation-skipping transfers.

I am not going to go into any great detail here, because this is an area of estate planning even qualified attorneys find complicated. In simple terms, however, assume Art has separate property worth over $2,000,000 and Ellie has nothing. If Art dies first, he can leave his estate to Ellie in such a way that both he and Ellie can make full use of the $1,000,000 exemption, and a total of $2,000,000 (plus appreciation) will pass to the little Dodgers without being taxed in Roger's estate.

But if Ellie dies first, her exemption will be lost and only $1,000,000 (plus appreciation) can pass to the little Dodgers tax free. After consulting independent legal counsel, Art may decide to make a lifetime gift to Ellie of $1,000,000, thereby assuring that both exemptions will be protected regardless of who dies first.

Although generation-skipping transfers provide dramatic tax savings, most taxpayers overlook this valuable planning tool.

In the next chapter, Art's ship finally comes in. But alas, too late.

CHAPTER 6

Thanks, But No Thanks

Last week the Artful Dodger's ship finally came in. His Aunt Agatha died at the age of 92 and left Art a tidy sum. Years ago this would have been cause for celebration (after Art had worked through his grief, of course.) But now, Art doesn't need the money. The inheritance will only increase the size of Art's estate and push him into a higher estate tax bracket.

Fortunately, Art has never been one to hold things in. And one evening at the local "tea room" Art complained to his clever attorney about his ship that came too late. Art's clever attorney suggested that Art drop in the next morning with a copy of Aunt Agatha's will to see if anything could be done.

Aunt Agatha's will contained the following gift to Art. "To my tightwad nephew, Artful Dodger, I give the sum of $100,000, if he survives me, and if he does not, I give this sum to his son, Roger."

Art's clever attorney explained that the solution to Art's problem was for Art to disclaim the $100,000 gift. A disclaimer is a legal way of saying, "Thanks, but no thanks." If Art disclaims the gift, the $100,000 will pass to Roger as if Art had died before his aunt. This is a once-in-a-lifetime opportunity for Art to make a tax-free gift to Roger without using up any of his $600,000 exemption.

Not surprisingly, however, Uncle Sam has established some strict requirements for disclaimers.

(1) Art's disclaimer must be in writing.

(2) Art must make the disclaimer within nine months of Aunt Agatha's death.

(3) Art cannot receive any benefits from the gift. For example, if Art had received the interest from the $100,000, he would be out of luck.

(4) Art cannot direct where the gift goes. But Aunt Agatha can. She has named Art's son, Roger, to receive the $100,000, if Art dies before her. Therefore, the gift will pass to Roger, if Art disclaims, without any direction from Art.

(5) The disclaimer must be irrevocable. Once the disclaimer is filed with the probate court:

> *Nor all your piety,*
> *nor wit shall lure it back*
> *to cancel half a line;*
> *nor all your tears*
> *wash out a word of it.*

So Art must reflect seriously on what he is about to do.

Art, upon reflection, decides it would be nice, after all, to have, say, $25,000 to take his wife, Ellie, on a long-promised cruise. No problem. Art can disclaim only $75,000 and keep the balance.

However, there is a flaw in the ointment (as Mrs. Malaprop would say). Remember the generation-skipping tax we talked about in the last chapter? Of course you do! Well, if Art makes a disclaimer, it's as if the gift passed directly from Aunt Agatha to Roger. Since Roger is more than one generation below Aunt Agatha, the gift could be subject to the confiscatory generation-skipping tax *if* Aunt Agatha has already used up her $1,000,000 generation-skipping tax exemption. Before making the disclaimer, Art should talk to Aunt Agatha's attorney to make sure he is not walking into a tax trap.

Next we'll look at one of the simplest tax saving devices which over time can yield huge rewards.

CHAPTER 7

The Mouse That Roared

Most of you probably know that every year you can give away $10,000 to each of any number of people tax free. What you may not fully appreciate is the magnitude of the tax savings that can be achieved by this simple device. This so-called annual exclusion is truly the mouse that roared.

For example, take our friend, the Artful Dodger. Art can give $10,000 to his son, Roger, and each of the six little Dodgers ($70,000 in all) each calendar year tax free. If Art's wife, Ellie, joins in the gift, together they can give $140,000.

In just a few years Art and Ellie can give away substantial sums of money that would otherwise have been taxed at their death.

There is one important restriction. The gifts must be of a "present interest" to qualify for the annual exclusion. In other words, the gifts must have no strings attached. Art will be quick to point out that one of his grandchildren is only 14. He is understandably reluctant to give $10,000 to a teenager who is likely to turn around and "invest" the money in the most expensive dirt bike in the county.

THE MINOR'S TRUST: Uncle Sam, who, for all we know, may have grandchildren of his own, has tried to solve Art's problem by creating what's known as a minor's trust. Art can now give money in trust to his teenage grandchild and still have the gift qualify for the annual exclusion.

The requirements of a minor's trust are simple. The trust money must be available for the benefit of the child until he or she reaches age 21, at which time the money must be payable to the child upon demand. Moreover, if the child dies before reaching age 21, the money is included in the minor's estate.

THE CALIFORNIA UNIFORM TRANSFERS TO MINORS ACT: Uncle Sam also allows for tax-free gifts to minors under the California Uniform Transfers to Minors Act. As in the case of the minor's trust, the money must be paid to the child at age 21 (age 25, if the gift is made at your death). The advantage of this type of gift is that it usually can be accomplished without the benefit of high-priced legal talent.

A CRUMMEY TRUST: In a famous tax case a taxpayer by the name of Mr. Crummey (no kidding, that's his real name) was not satisfied with either of these two options. He was horrified at the thought of his children getting their hands on the trust money at age 21. So Mr. Crummey and his clever attorney drafted a different kind of trust.

It provided that when Mr. Crummey transferred $10,000 to a child's trust, the child had the right to take the $10,000 out the same year, thus satisfying the requirement that the gift be of a present interest. If the child didn't, the money would remain in the trust until the child was 35. (Mr. Crummey could have chosen any age.) Mr. Crummey never intended that a child exercise his or her right of withdrawal. And since Mr. Crummey could disinherit any child who did, it's a good bet that Mr. Crummey got his way.

Mr. Crummey's trust has been upheld by the courts and is now a popular estate planning device. You can hardly blame attorneys for preferring the minor's trust, however. For it can hardly be good for business to have a client running around town telling all his friends that his attorney drafted a "Crummey Trust."

In the next chapter we will look at three different types of gifts—small, medium, and large.

CHAPTER 8

Gifts in Three Different Sizes

Making gifts, especially to family members, is one of the most effective ways to save estate taxes. Since the Artful Dodger's path to earthly bliss is through tax avoidance, he is anxious to learn all he can about all three sizes of gifts.

ANNUAL EXCLUSION GIFTS: As you know, each calendar year Art can give $10,000 to his son, Roger, and to each of Roger's six children tax free (or to anyone else, for that matter). Art and his wife, Ellie, together, can give twice this amount. What you may not know is that Art can also pay an unlimited amount of the medical expenses and tuition for Roger and his children. For these gifts to be tax free, however, Art must pay the money directly to the medical care provider or the educational institution.

Warning! If Art has executed a living trust, he must keep in mind that Art, the individual, is not the same person as Art, the trustee. The former is entitled to the $10,000 annual exclusion; the latter is not. Hence, Art should take the $10,000 out of the trust *before* making any gifts to Roger or the little Dodgers. If‘ he makes gifts directly from the trust, Uncle Sam may deny the exclusion.

But what if Art becomes incompetent and loses the capacity to make a gift? On the advice of his clever attorney, Art has executed a durable general power of attorney giving his agent the power to make annual exclusion gifts to family members. If Art becomes incompetent, his trustee (probably Ellie) can transfer $10,000 out of the trust to his agent (probably also Ellie) who can then make the gift on Art's behalf.

GIFTS PROTECTED BY THE EXEMPTION: Like every other taxpayer, Art was born with a bellybutton and a $600,000 exemption. This means Art can give away during his life or at his death a total of $600,000 tax free. Art used to view this exemption much as a squirrel views nuts stored for the winter. The last thing he wanted to do was to consume it. After a chat with his clever attorney, however, Art had a change of heart.

For example, Art owns a summer cabin worth $150,000. If Art gives the cabin to Roger, he will use up $150,000 of his exemption, true. But the cabin *plus* any increase in its value will be removed from Art's estate. If the cabin appreciates $100,000 between the date of the gift and date of Art's death, estate taxes on this $100,000 will have been saved.

GIFTS IN EXCESS OF THE EXEMPTION: Let's assume Art was so impressed with his clever attorney's advice that he used up his *entire* $600,000 exemption by making gifts to Roger and the little Dodgers. To make it simple let's also assume that Art is in a 50% estate and gift tax bracket.

If Art now gives Roger $100,000, he will have to pay a gift tax of $50,000. It will therefore cost Art $150,000 to make a $100,000 gift. If Art doesn't make the gift but, instead, leaves Roger $150,000 in his will, at Art's death his estate will pay a tax of $75,000 on that $150,000. In this case, Roger will be left with only $75,000.

How can this be? I told you earlier that tax rates for gifts and estates are the same. This is the truth, but it's not the whole truth. Uncle Sam doesn't tax the tax on gifts. But he does tax the tax on estates. As a result, it is cheaper to give your estate away during your life than at death.

BE CAREFUL! Art must take something very important into account before making a gift. Let's look again at Art's summer cabin, for which he paid $10,000 many years ago. If Art gives the summer cabin to Roger, Roger will take over Art's $10,000 basis. If Roger sells the cabin, he will pay capital gains tax on everything he receives over $10,000.

If, on the other hand, Art bequeaths the cabin to Roger, Roger will receive a new basis equal to the value of the cabin at Art's death, say $250,000. If Roger sells the cabin for $250,000, he will pay no capital gains tax.

The solution is for Art to give Roger assets that have not appreciated (such as cash, bonds, or his Costco stock) or assets that Roger is not likely to sell during his lifetime (such as the summer cabin). Likewise, Art should hold onto assets that have gone up in value.

As a final caution, before making *any* large gifts to Roger, Art should dust off Shakespeare's Collected Works and reread *King Lear*.

As a lad, Uncle Sam napped through Euclidian geometry. We'll see next just how this can work to your advantage.

CHAPTER 9

Non Euclidian Gifts

Uncle Sam has some rather embarrassing gaps in his formal education—geometry being one. (In fact, if the truth be known, Uncle Sam thinks Euclid refers to a tribe of North American Eskimos.) Therefore, he never grasped the basic Euclidian hypothesis that the whole is equal to the sum of its parts. Uncle Sam's loss can be your gain, especially when it comes to making annual exclusion gifts of large assets, such as the family business or a vacation home, to younger generations. Allow me to explain.

Let's assume Art and Ellie own a business that has been recently appraised at $200,000. The Dodgers want to transfer the business to Roger so it will not be taxed in their estate. As I hope you know by now, Art and Ellie can give Roger $20,000 each year tax free. Your lightening mathematical sense no doubt tells you the Dodgers can give Roger only 10% of the business in the first year. Your lightning mathematical sense is wrong.

MINORITY DISCOUNT: Remarkably, Uncle Sam allows the value of a minority interest to be discounted. The theory is that the minority interest is worth less because it is subject to the control of the majority owners. This is true even if the majority owners, to wit: Art and Ellie, happen to be the parents of the minority owner, to wit: Roger.

How much less? That is for an appraiser to determine. A 20% discount for a minority interest is not unusual. In that case, the Dodgers could give more than 10% of the business to Roger the first year and still be within the $20,000 annual exclusion. And that's not all.

MARKETABILITY DISCOUNT: As in many families, there is a certain amount of friction between Ellie and her daughter-in-law (Roger's wife). In fact, Ellie has mentioned with great feeling (not to mention alliteration) that she would "first fry in hell" before letting Roger's wife get her "fat little fingers" into the family business.

Therefore, the Dodgers have asked their clever attorney to draft an agreement giving them the right to buy back Roger's interest at a set price if he dies before they do. This buyout agreement eliminates the risk that Roger's wife will get involved in the business. It also further reduces the value of the gift to Roger, since this restriction makes Roger's interest less marketable. This in turn allows the Dodgers to give to Roger an even greater percentage of the business and still stay within their $20,000 annual exclusion.

THE ENTITY: The form of the Dodgers' business is important. For example, if the business is conducted as general partnership, the gift to Roger will make him a general partner. As such he will have unlimited personal liability for partnership debts. Roger may be reluctant to accept this risk. Roger will also have a voice in the management of the business. Art may be unwilling to accept this risk.

If the business is a limited partnership, by law Roger can have no management authority. If the business is a corporation, Art can limit Roger's authority by giving him only non-voting stock. In both cases, and in the case of a limited liability company as well, Roger's liability will be limited.

Do you own life insurance? Maybe you shouldn't. To find out, read on.

CHAPTER 10

Life Insurance: Get Rid of It

Let's talk about life insurance. Wait! Don't turn the page! I am not trying to sell you anything. There are things you must know about life insurance if you are serious about saving taxes. So read on.

Years ago the Artful Dodger purchased a $100,000 policy of life insurance naming his son, Roger, as the beneficiary. Art is the owner of the policy. He is also the insured, since it his death that will trigger the payoff of $100,000. Roger, as the beneficiary, will get the money.

Art is shocked to discover that on his death the $100,000 will be taxed in his estate. What is especially galling to Art is that he purchased life insurance to pay estate taxes, not to create them. In addition to a couple of aspirin, Art needs some basic tax advice.

There is a simple solution to Art's problem: Art should give the insurance policy to Roger. Art will still be the insured and Roger will still be the beneficiary. Only the ownership of the policy will change.

"Do you mean to tell me that insurance on my life can be owned by someone other than me?" Art asks. Absolutely.

"Isn't that a taxable gift?" Art persists. Probably not. Though the proceeds from the policy at Art's death will be $100,000, the policy's value while Art is alive is relatively small. If it is under $10,000, Art can give the policy to Roger tax free under the annual exclusion. (Remember the annual exclusion?) Together, Art and his wife can give Roger an insurance policy worth $20,000 tax free.

Now for the really exciting news! At Art's death, since Art no longer owns the life insurance, the $100,000 will pass to Roger tax free—that is, free of estate tax and free of income tax.

"So what's the hitch?" asks Art, who has been on guard ever since he lost his shirt in a tax shelter having something to do with recycling used dental floss. Only two hitches: First, Art must survive the gift by three years or the entire $100,000 will be taxed in his estate. Second, Roger, not Art, should pay future insurance premiums or some of the $100,000 will be taxed in Art's estate. (Art, however, can give Roger the money to pay the premiums.)

Art can go one step further. He can name Roger's children as beneficiaries and then give the policy to the children. In this way he can transfer $100,000 to his grandchildren tax free. The $100,000 is thus taxed in neither Art's *nor* Roger's estate. This may present a problem if there is a chance Roger's children will cash in the policy the first time they walk past a store window displaying roller blades.

Art can solve this problem by transferring the policy to an irrevocable trust for the benefit of his grandchildren or to a custodian for the benefit of the minors under the California Uniform Transfers to Minors Act. (Art must be sure not to name himself as either trustee or custodian, however.)

In most cases, transferring ownership of insurance policies can be accomplished easily and without the need of a lot of high-priced legal talent. In fact, a call to your insurance agent is all it usually takes to obtain the forms necessary to make the change. And the tax savings can be dramatic!

In the next chapter I'm going to reveal something very personal about Uncle Sam that may shock you. It may also save you taxes.

CHAPTER 11

Gambling with Uncle Sam

You may find this hard to believe, but Uncle Sam is an incurable gambler. (Remember, you read it here first.) He has joined gamblers anonymous and tried numerous expensive cures, (all at taxpayer expense), but to no avail. Fortunately, taxpayers can sometimes win bets with Uncle Sam. So if you too occasionally like to "play the ponies," pay close attention to what I'm about to tell you.

Several years ago, just when it appeared Uncle Sam had finally kicked the habit, he fell off the wagon with a thud and offered taxpayers a betting proposition that many found irresistible. Of course, the Artful Dodger jumped at the chance to win a nickel off Uncle Sam. Here's how.

Art owns a residence worth $500,000. If he leaves the residence to his son, Roger, it will be taxed in Art's estate when he dies. Instead of leaving the residence to Roger, Uncle Sam allows Art to give the residence to a qualified personal residence trust (known by tax experts and in gambling circles as a "QPRT"). Art gets to live in the residence for as many years as he chooses. Let's say Art chooses eight years. After eight years, ownership of the residence must pass to Roger.

Here's the gamble: Assuming Art is age 60, if he lives eight years or more he wins. Art has made a gift to Roger of the residence but the value of the gift is discounted to $378,000 to take into account the eight years Art can continue to live there. Sure, Art has used up $378,000 of his $600,000 exemption. But in return he has removed a $500,000 residence, plus any appreciation occurring after the gift, from his taxable estate.

If Art doesn't survive the eight years, Uncle Sam wins. The residence falls back into Art's estate where it is taxed at 100% of its value on the date of Art's death. It's as if the QPRT had never existed.

The trick, obviously, is for Art to guess right in choosing the number of years he can live in the residence. The more years he chooses, the more the value of the gift is discounted. For example, if Art had chosen 10 years, the gift would have been valued at $350,000. If Art gets too piggy, however, and picks 15 years, he may not survive that long, and he will lose his bet with Uncle Sam.

Art, always the skeptic, has a number of questions:

"What if I survive the eight years but don't want to leave my residence?"

In that case, Art can continue to live in the residence as long as he is willing to pay Roger a fair rent.

"Will this plan work with any other assets?"

Yes, Art can also put one other residence, such as his mountain cabin, into a separate QPRT. But that's it—only two per customer.

"What if I later decide to sell my residence?"

The trust can sell Art's residence and reinvest the proceeds in a replacement residence. The trustee has two years, at most, however, to buy a replacement residence. If the trustee doesn't, the trust will terminate and the sales proceeds will be taxed in Art's estate.

In the next chapter I will answer the question, "Do you need a will?" Hint: When an attorney asks this question, you can bet the farm it is purely rhetorical.

CHAPTER 12

To Will or Not to Will

So far we have discussed some pretty exotic tax-planning techniques. In this chapter, we're going back to basics. Not everybody has an estate large enough to require tax planning. (Nor does everyone, like the Artful Dodger, have a borderline personality when it comes to trying to avoid taxes.)

Let's start with the most fundamental question of all.

DO I NEED A WILL? If you die without a will, you die "intestate." No, this doesn't mean all your earthly booty is forfeited to the state. It does mean your property passes by "intestate succession." This is the law that, in effect, writes your will for you if you don't have one. It provides for the distribution of your estate to the people whom the state assumes you would have chosen.

For example, if you are married, your half of the community property passes to your surviving spouse and your separate property passes to both your surviving spouse and your children. If you are single, without children, your property passes to your parents equally.

This may not be so bad. But it also may not be what you want.

WHO'S IN CHARGE: In your will you can name your representative. This is the person who will have the responsibility of administering your estate. And you can waive the requirement for a bond. (A bond is like an insurance policy that protects your estate if the representative disappears in your Ferrari Testarossa.)

You should waive bond if you have complete trust in your chosen representative. This is important since bonds are expensive. (Today, a bond on a $750,000 estate costs about $950 per year.)

If you die intestate, your representative will be appointed by the court and bond may be required even if your representative is a family member.

The choice of your representative can be important. Normally it will be a family member. However, if Thanksgiving in your family has come to be known as the "annual brawl," you should consider someone outside the family or even a professional representative such as a bank trust department.

ALTERNATIVES TO A WILL: Not all property passes by your will. For example, property held in joint tenancy passes to the surviving joint tenant outside your will. Therefore, if you hold title to Bleakacre in joint tenancy with your girlfriend, Marilyn, at your death it will pass automatically to her. (If you also have left Bleakacre in your will to your other girlfriend, Carolyn, you have set the stage for the type of nasty lawsuit that allows attorneys to send their kids to private schools.)

Retirement benefits, life insurance, and some investments (like government bonds) that are payable at your death to another person will not pass by your will. Nor will bank accounts held in trust for another or, of course, assets held in a living trust.

So it *is* possible for you to direct where your property will go without having a will. This is risky, however. For if the other joint tenant of Bleakacre or the beneficiary of your life insurance dies before you (or in a common disaster with you), this property will pass by intestate succession at your death.

In the next chapter, I will tell you something that just may help you win your next bar bet.

CHAPTER 13

The Living Trust: Fact and Fiction

Perhaps you've seen the ads similar to the one that has appeared in newspapers throughout California. In the ad a self-styled "money expert" invites you to attend his "Money Power Workshop." Here he promises to show you how living trusts can "reduce or eliminate estate taxes." This is pure eyewash.

THE FICTION: Living trusts save estate taxes. Not so! Living trusts do *not* save estate taxes. These money experts, along with others who make their living selling living trusts, like washing detergent, often confuse the public by making this claim.

The truth is, a living trust *is* a valuable estate planning tool you should consider. But not for the wrong reasons.

THE FACT: A living trust is a will substitute. In the typical living trust, an individual transfers all of his or her property to himself or herself as trustee of a living trust. Although a living trust doesn't save taxes, it *does* avoid probate.

Probate is the judicial process for the orderly distribution of an estate. The problem with probate is probate fees.

Your attorney and your executor are each entitled to a probate fee, which is set by statute. The fee is the same for each. Your executor, if a member of your family, will probably waive the fee. Therefore, in most cases only the attorney's fee should concern you. For example, in a $500,000 dollar estate the probate fee is $11,150. (As we will see in a few paragraphs, however, this fee is not carved in marble.)

Attorneys may also charge extraordinary fees for services that go beyond the normal probate duties. Most judges, however, are loathe to allow extraordinary fees unless the attorney can make a compelling case that they are justified.

In addition to probate avoidance, a living trust offers other advantages. It affords an economical alternative to a conservatorship. In the event of your future incapacity, the successor trustee *you* name, rather than a court appointed conservator, will take over handling your affairs.

If you own real property in another state, a living trust offers a simple method of transferring the property at your death without the need of setting up a probate in a foreign state.

A living trust costs more than a will because it is a more complicated document and because, after executing the trust, you must transfer your assets into it. In a recent survey of attorneys specializing in estate planning, the average cost of wills for a married couple was approximately $350 while the average cost of a living trust was approximately $1,000.

Believe it or not, probate actually has some advantages. For example, in some cases probate affords a simpler way to transfer assets to your beneficiaries. It also provides an opportunity to save income taxes by choosing a fiscal year.

A MODEST PROPOSAL: For those who are not sure they want a living trust, there is a middle ground. In your will you can advise your executor that probate fees, though set by statute, are negotiable. You can instruct your executor to negotiate probate fees before hiring a probate attorney. You can even point out that your executor need not hire the attorney who drafted your will to probate your estate. For a well organized estate, your executor should be able to negotiate a 30% to 50% reduction of the normal probate fee.

Next let's look inside an estate planner's toolbox to see the types of tools that will fix future problems.

CHAPTER 14

Your Estate Planning Toolbox

In this chapter we're going to take a break from taxes. (Buck up! We'll return to them soon enough.) Instead, I'm going to tell you about various documents you may want to include in your estate plan. Think of these documents as tools in your estate planning toolbox. At least one of these tools may be just the right thing to fix a future problem.

DURABLE POWER OF ATTORNEY FOR HEALTH CARE: This document (Appendix C) allows you to appoint the person of your choice to make health care decisions for you if you are unable to do so. At the same time, you can designate that your life not be artificially prolonged if your condition is irreversible, or, alternatively, that every measure be undertaken to keep you alive. You may also consent to the donation of your body parts for medical or scientific purposes. The advantage of this document is that it invests the person of *your* choice with the power to monitor and control the course of your medical treatment when you can't. If there is someone to whom you are willing to delegate this authority, do it!

DIRECTIVE TO PHYSICIANS: This document, sometimes referred to as a living will, (Appendix D) is useful if there is nobody to whom you want to delegate your health care decisions. It directs your physician to withhold life sustaining treatment if you are in an irreversible coma.

DURABLE GENERAL POWER OF ATTORNEY: This document (Appendix E) appoints another person to conduct your affairs for you.

You can choose to have it take effect immediately or only in the event of your future incompetency. In cases of temporary disability, it is an economical alternative to a conservatorship.

If you have a living trust, you should execute a power of attorney too. It can be used to transfer assets you might have overlooked into the trust if you become unable to do so.

COMMUNITY PROPERTY AFFIDAVIT: This document (Appendix F) converts assets held in joint tenancy to community property. In chapter 19 we will discuss the advantages of holding property that has gone up in value as community property. This is one of the most important things you will learn in this book!

Before 1985 a husband and wife could change the way property was held by oral agreement. Therefore, after the death of a spouse, you could sometimes convince Uncle Sam that property acquired before 1985 and held in joint tenancy was changed to community property by oral agreement. If the property was acquired after 1985, Uncle Sam insists that any change from joint tenancy to community property be in writing. This simple affidavit is all you need. And it can save you substantial income taxes!

NOMINATION OF CONSERVATOR: A conservatorship is a judicial proceeding in which the court appoints an individual or an institution to handle your affairs if you are unable to do so yourself. Did you know you can nominate your own conservator even if you may never need a conservatorship? You can also nominate a conservator in your durable power of attorney for health care.

In most conservatorships the conservator must post a bond. The bond protects the conservatorship from loss if the conservator takes a powder to Mexico with the conservatorship assets. Bonds can be expensive. Therefore, when your nominee is a trusted relative or a close family friend, you may wish to waive the bond requirement in your nomination (Appendix G).

Are you charitably disposed? In tax planning, though good deeds are their own reward, Uncle Sam sweetens the pot.

CHAPTER 15

Doing Well by Doing Good

The other day The Artful Dodger had quite a shock. His clever attorney suggested the possibility of Art's making a gift to charity. Since Art's prior charitable generosity has been limited to buying single boxes of Girl Scout cookies, Art wondered if the suggestion might be the result of a two-martini lunch. But by the time Art's clever attorney had finished explaining the tax advantages of charitable giving, Art's cold heart had turned downright eleemosynary.

THE PROBLEM: Art owns a rental unit worth $500,000 that he purchased for peanuts many years ago. Unfortunately, it brings in only $1250 in monthly rent. Art wants to sell the property and invest the proceeds in high-interest utility stocks. After paying capital gains tax on the sale, however, Art will have only $350,000 left to invest. To add insult to injury, on Art's death the $350,000 will be taxed in Art's estate. Art's son, Roger, will end up receiving a measly $210,000.

THE CHARITABLE SOLUTION: There is an alternative to this depressing scenario, especially if Art would prefer to see tax dollars flow to charity instead of into Uncle Sam's pocket. For Uncle Sam is uncharacteristically charitable to the taxpayer who is, himself, charitable.

Instead of selling his rental, Art can set up a charitable remainder trust. Art then transfers the rental property into the trust. When the trust sells the property, it pays *no* capital gains tax and the entire $500,000 can be invested in those high-yield utility stocks. Art can direct that the trustee pay him a stated amount from the trust (say 7 per cent) annually. He also can direct, at his death, that the trustee continue to pay this amount to his wife, Ellie, for her life. He can even require that, at Ellie's death, the trustee pay this amount to their son, Roger, for his life. But on Roger's death, what's left in the trust must pass to charity.

The primary advantage of a charitable remainder trust is that Art can invest the *entire* sales proceeds from his rental unit for the benefit of his family without any attrition due to capital gains tax.

There are other benefits as well. Art can take a charitable deduction on his income tax return, which will shelter some of the money the trust pays him each year. The amount of the deduction depends on the value of the eventual gift to charity as computed by Uncle Sam. For example, if the trust terminates on Art's death, the deduction is bigger than if the trust continues on for the life of Ellie and Roger. And if Art can't use up all the deduction in one year, he can carry it forward up to five years.

Also, the trust will pay no capital gains tax on the sale of the assets in which it has invested. Thus, if the trust sells Intermittent Gas and Electricity, Inc. at a gain, the entire proceeds can be reinvested.

Art is still worried that Roger may need more cash. No problem. Art can use some of the money he receives from the trust to buy a life insurance policy on Art's life, naming Roger as the beneficiary. In fact, Art can transfer ownership of the policy to Roger. That way, at Art's death the proceeds will not be taxable in Art's estate.

One other advantage pleases Art, although he won't admit it. He and Ellie most likely will receive immediate public recognition for their generosity. All of which is better than a few stale Girl Scout cookies.

Next it's back to the basics of charitable giving.

CHAPTER 16

Doing Still Better

Look around you. The opportunities for charitable giving are every-where. Children are going hungry, libraries are closed on weekends, high schools are without orchestras or computer labs. Not that any of this does much to soften the obdurate heart of the Artful Dodger. But when Art considers the tax savings that can result from charitable gifts, that same heart softens ever so slightly.

Whether you are truly motivated by a desire to make this world a better place or, like Art, interested mostly in saving taxes, you should know the basics of charitable giving.

LIFETIME GIFTS: As you all know, charitable gifts of cash are fully de-ductible. The fair market value of noncash gifts is also deductible. (Certain limitations apply to so few of us that I am not going to bore you with the details.) This gives rise to opportunities in the case of appreciated assets.

Years ago Art made a killing in the stock market. In just a few years, his 100 shares of Black, Inc. went from $100 to $10,000. Art has heard a rumor that Black, Inc. may soon be showing some red ink and he wants to bail out.

To buy peace at home, he also feels compelled to make a charitable gift to Ellie's favorite charity. If he sells the stock, he will pay income tax on the gain of $9,900, which at Art's tax bracket of 39% will leave him $6,039. If he then donates this sum to charity, the tax saving on this gift will amount to only $2,355. If, on the other hand, Art simply gives the Black, Inc. stock to Ellie's favorite charity, he will avoid pay-ing any income tax on the gain and can deduct the entire $10,000. Art's tax saving now will be $3,900. The point is simple: If you have in-vested wisely (or luckily), give the asset, not the proceeds.

GIFTS OF LIFE INSURANCE: Art has an old life insurance policy on his life for $25,000, naming Ellie as the beneficiary. Ellie doesn't really need insurance protection any more. If Art gives the policy to charity, he can deduct the value of the policy from his taxes and the charity will get the proceeds at Art's death.

Ellie thinks this is a great idea since her favorite charity will eventually end up with $25,000. Art thinks it's a great idea too, because of the tax deduction and because, frankly, the insurance on his life wasn't doing *him* much good anyway.

And there's one more advantage. A gift of life insurance to charity increases the likelihood that, at your death, your survivors will be truly grieved.

GIFTS AT DEATH: The value of a bequest to charity is deductible for estate tax purposes. When Ellie and Art are both gone, Ellie wants to leave $100,000 to charity. If she is in a 50% estate tax bracket, Uncle Sam will, in effect, contribute half the gift.

Ellie would like to leave an even larger amount to charity but also wants to be sure that her son, Roger, and the little Dodgers are adequately provided for. She and Art can make the bequest to a charitable remainder trust. The trust can be set up so it makes regular monthly payments to Roger, and on Roger's death, to the little Dodgers. Only on the death of the last little Dodger will what's left pass to charity. The good news is that Uncle Sam still allows an estate tax deduction for the discounted value of the gift that will eventually go to charity.

I don't mean to scare you, but in the next chapter there will be a test of your probate I.Q.

CHAPTER 17

Test Your Probate I.Q.

In a recent survey average Americans were given the following multiple-choice test:

"Probate is:

   a. A really nasty toxin.

   b. A sexually transmitted disease.

   c. The judicial process for the orderly distribution of an estate."

A majority of respondents guessed wrong and no wonder. You no doubt have heard probate talked about as if it were the fifth horseman of the apocalypse. Yet, if you're like most people, you probably don't have much of an idea just what probate is.

For starters, the following property does not have to be probated:

(a) Property held in joint tenancy.

(b) Life insurance proceeds (unless you named your probate estate as the beneficiary).

(c) Assets, such as retirement accounts (like IRAs) and government bonds, that are payable on death to a person you name.

(d) All assets passing outright from one spouse to another.

(e) Assets held in a living trust.

The rest of your property is subject to probate. Let's take a short stroll through probate to see what it's really all about.

A probate proceeding is started by the person you named in your will as your representative. If you didn't get around to making a will, just about anybody can start the proceeding (even one of your creditors) but preference is given to your spouse and your relatives.

The person seeking to be your representative files a petition for probate in the superior court. He or she then publishes a "Notice to Administer Estate" in a local newspaper, which informs your creditors that they must file their claims and sets the date for the first hearing. This notice must also be sent to all the beneficiaries named in your will, as well as to your next of kin.

At the first hearing, the judge appoints the person who will have the responsibility of managing your estate. This person is called an executor if he was named in your will, or an administrator if you died without a will. (If the person is a she and you are either a Latin scholar or a snob, she is called an executrix or an administratrix.) The term "personal representative" covers both.

Unless your will is challenged, the judge will admit your will to probate and order letters of administration issued to your personal representative. These letters are your representative's written authority to act for the estate. Your creditors have four months from the date these letters are issued to file a claim against your estate for money due, or they will be out of luck.

This cutoff of creditors' claims is an important benefit of probate. For example, if you are a doctor, a lawyer, or other professional, malpractice claims that are not filed on time are forever barred. Moreover, your representative can choose to probate both halves of the community property, thus protecting all community property, such as the family residence, from future claims.

Just what exactly does your representative do to probate your estate? Read on, MacDuff.

CHAPTER 18

More About Probate

I know a lot of you readers, in a state of nail-biting anxiety, have rushed ahead to learn more about the probate process. Here, then, is the second installment.

Your representative's first task is to inventory the property of the estate and have it appraised, usually by the probate referee. These values are used on your estate tax return if one is required.

These values also establish the new tax basis of all estate assets. For example, the Carmel cottage you purchased for $50,000 (your original basis) will get a new basis of $500,000, the value at the date of your death. Your beneficiaries will pay capital gains tax on *only* the sales proceeds over $500,000.

It used to be every time your representative wanted to do anything important, he or she had to go to court for authority. Now your representative takes most actions such as selling property, investing estate assets, entering into contracts, and the like without going to court. Instead, he or she needs only to notify your beneficiaries in advance of any such action. If none objects, he or she can go ahead.

However, your representative may run into a problem that requires court assistance. For example, let's say your will provides, "To my good friend, Art Dodger, I leave $10,000 so he can take good care of my pit bull, 'Fluffy.'" Unfortunately, Fluffy trotted off to his reward years ago. Art claims he should get the money, anyway. Your children, who get the rest of your estate, are adamant: "No 'Fluffy,' no $10,000."

Your representative can request the court to instruct him or her just what to do. Probate judges, who handle scores of probate cases each week, are adept at solving problems such as this. And your representative, in following the judge's instruction, is protected from personal liability.

During probate your representative receives all income, pays all expenses, invests surplus cash, and generally manages your estate. He or she also files your last personal income tax return along with your estate's income tax returns, known as fiduciary returns.

If your gross estate exceeds $600,000, your representative also must file an estate tax return within nine months of your death. After the time for filing creditors' claims has expired and after your estate tax return has been filed, your estate can be closed.

Your representative then files a petition for distribution in the probate court. Unless waived by the beneficiaries, your representative must attach an itemized accounting showing all assets at the beginning of the probate and at its end, all income and expenses, and all gains and losses on sales. The tricky part, of course, is that the accounting must balance.

The representative also requests approval of his or her fees and the probate attorney's fees. Your representative and the probate attorney are each entitled to a probate fee that, for estates under $1,000,000, is equal to 2% of the gross value of the estate plus $1,150. The probate fee is 1% on anything over $1,000,000 and (I realize this is getting somewhat academic) $1/2$% on anything over $10,000,000.

Your representative, especially if a family member, will probably waive this fee. Attorney's fees also may be less than the probate fee if negotiated at the beginning of the probate proceeding.

Finally, your representative sets out how the estate will be distributed. Once this petition is approved, your representative will distribute your estate and be discharged.

In the next chapter you will learn how one simple, inexpensive affidavit can save you lots of income tax.

CHAPTER 19

One More Reason to Live in California

The way in which you and your spouse hold title to property has significant income tax consequences. In fact, Uncle Sam, in a rare outburst of generosity, has made tax savings available in community property states, like California, that are not available elsewhere. To illustrate how this beneficence can save you taxes, we will turn again to the Artful Dodger, who, you recall, has raised tax avoidance to an art form.

CAPITAL GAINS TAX: You will recall that years ago Art had the foresight to buy 100 shares of Black, Inc. for $100 which has soared in value to $10,000. (If you don't, I'm sure Art will be happy to regale you with the details.) If Art sells the stock, he will pay income tax on the difference between the original cost of $100 (known as his cost basis) and the sales price of $10,000.

If Art dies owning these shares of Black, Inc., however, his cost basis is "stepped up" to the stock's value (say $10,000) at his death. If Black, Inc. is sold for $10,000 after Art's death, no income tax is payable.

If, instead, Art and his wife, Ellie, own Black, Inc. as joint tenants, upon *either's* death, the basis will be stepped up but only as to one half the difference between the cost basis of $100 and the value at death of $10,000. The new basis will be $5,050 ($100 plus $4,950). If the surviving spouse sells the stock for $10,000, the remaining $4850 is taxed.

When Art and Ellie told their clever attorney they owned Black, Inc. (along with their residence and other appreciated assets) in joint tenancy, their clever attorney wouldn't let them out the door until they had signed a community property affidavit (Appendix F) stating that all these joint tenancy assets were really community property. As a result, the situation will be dramatically different on the death of the first spouse. The basis of the stock, as if it had been sprinkled with pixie dust, will be stepped up to $10,000 regardless of whether Art or Ellie is the first to die. If the surviving spouse sells the stock for $10,000, *no* income tax is payable.

Holding title as community property has one other advantage. On Art's death, for example, since community property assets get a stepped-up basis, Ellie will not have to go rummaging through Art's business records (located in a cardboard box, God knows where) to try to figure out the original cost of each asset.

HOW TO SAVE IT: Here are some ways you can take advantage of these rules and save income taxes.

(1) Do you and your spouse own a residence? If so, pull out the deed to your residence. Chances are you and your spouse hold title as joint tenants. (This is probably because the person at the title company told you to take title this way.) If your residence has gone up in value, convert it to community property along with any other appreciated joint tenancy property. Just like Art and Ellie you can do this by executing a simple community property affidavit. This way the surviving spouse will get a full step up in basis on the death of the first spouse to die.

Be careful, however. If you own joint tenancy assets that have gone down in value, you may not want to change them to community property. A joint tenancy asset that has depreciated gives the surviving spouse a bigger income tax loss than in the case of an asset held as community property. In this case, it is better not to execute an all-inclusive community property affidavit but, instead, to transfer to community property only those assets that have appreciated.

(2) Do you and your spouse each own appreciated separate property? If so, each of you should transfer separate property of equal value to community property. Then no matter which of you dies first, the survivor will get a full step up in basis on all the converted property.

(3) What if you own appreciated separate property but your spouse doesn't? Consider transferring it to community property even if your spouse cannot match the transfer with separate property of his or her own. If your spouse dies before you, you will get a step up in basis on the community property that was formerly your separate property.

Obviously, this strategy raises considerations that go beyond tax planning. You will be making a transfer of your separate property to community property that once made is irrevocable. If you and your spouse divorce, you will doubtless come to regard this bit of tax planning as unenlightened.

In the next chapter we will treat with a subject that most of us would just as soon avoid—planning for our untimely death.

CHAPTER 20

Providing for Your Orphans

Small wonder we procrastinate when it comes to planning our estates. To plan an estate is to concede to our mortality; it is to hear at our back "time's winged chariot hurrying near."

Worse yet, to plan well we must advert to unpleasant eventualities, such as an untimely death, that may leave young children orphaned. Plan we must, however, for the consequences of not doing so can be unfortunate.

GUARDIANSHIP OF THE PERSON: As long as either you or your spouse is living, the surviving spouse will most likely provide for the needs of any minor children. On the death of the surviving spouse, however, or if both you and your spouse die in a common disaster, the court will appoint a guardian of the person of your minor children. This guardian will have the responsibility of raising your children. In your will you should designate the person or persons you want to assume this task. Remember, if you appoint a married couple as guardians, you should state what is to happen if the couple separates. And you should discuss the guardianship with the persons you name to make sure they are willing to accept the responsibility.

GUARDIANSHIP OF THE ESTATE: If you leave property outright to minor children either by will or joint tenancy or through life insurance, the court will appoint a guardian of your children's estate who will have the responsibility of managing your children's property until they reach age 18.

You can designate this person in your will. Estate guardianships, however, have disadvantages. For example, a guardianship bond may be required, which can be expensive. Also, the guardian must obtain court approval before making any sales, investments, or distributions, which can add to the cost.

Most importantly, the estate must be distributed to your child at age 18. And if your child dies before age 18, the estate will be distributed to the child's heirs. This may not be what you want.

GIFTS IN TRUST: Is there an alternative to a guardianship of the estate? Yes. In your will or your living trust, you can set up a trust for your children. A trust has two major advantages:

First, you have great flexibility in just how you want the trust administered and distributed. For example, you can establish a separate trust for each child that distributes one half of the property when your child reaches 25 and the balance at age 30. Or you can provide for a single trust to be held for the benefit of all your children until the youngest child reaches 21.

Second, if a child dies before the trust terminates, you can direct to whom distribution of the child's share should be made—to the child's spouse, for example, or the child's children, or your other children.

GIFT TO CUSTODIAN: A simple alternative to a trust can also avoid the necessity of a guardianship. You can make a gift in your will to a custodian for your child under the California Uniform Transfers to Minors Act. The custodian you appoint can manage your child's estate without any court supervision. This means no bonds, no accountings, and probably no attorney's fees. And you can delay payment to your child until age 25.

SPECIAL NEEDS TRUST: If you have a disabled child who is receiving or likely to receive public benefit assistance, there is an added concern. A bequest to the child may disqualify the child from receiving that assistance. Consider leaving the child's bequest to a special needs trust. In this trust, the trustee's authority is limited to providing your child with only those benefits *not* paid for by public assistance.

The result is that Medi-Cal, for example, cannot consider the assets of the trust in determining your child's eligibility. And the trustee can provide your child with important assistance not covered by Medi-Cal, such as a specially equipped vehicle, dental care, rehabilitation, or even a vacation.

In the next chapter we are going to travel to some pretty exotic islands. The question is, should we take all our earthly possessions with us?

CHAPTER 21

Go Offshore, Young Man

Our favorite worrywart, the Artful Dodger, has been losing sleep, not to mention hair, lately. Now that he has scads of money, he is obsessed by the idea that someone, besides Uncle Sam, will try to take it away from him. Art has read about juries awarding great gobbets of cash for injuries not much worse than a hangnail. Lately, in the watch hours of the morning, he's had dark visions of his home being sold at sheriff's auction, of his Stairmaster being repossessed.

Art was, therefore, all ears when a golfing buddy boasted that he, along with all of the other "smart-money" guys, had "gone offshore" with their assets.

Art immediately rushed off to his clever attorney to see if he too could join the ranks of the smart-money guys.

GOING OFFSHORE: Indeed, so-called Foreign Protection of Asset Trusts have generated much interest lately. So much so that a latter-day Horace Greeley might be heard to say, "Go offshore, young man, go offshore." For which of us isn't beguiled by the dream of sitting on a beach next to a stack of hard-earned dollars, watching our creditors pile up on the reef? Unfortunately, as Art learned, for most of us the dream may have a morning after.

The idea of an offshore trust is simple. The grantor creates a trust under the laws of a foreign country, transferring his or her assets into the trust. The trust makes distributions to family members such as his or her spouse and their children. At the end of the term of the trust, the grantor can either take the assets back or, if creditors are still lurking, extend the trust.

FRAUDULENT CONVEYANCES: The trust does not save taxes. Its sole objective is to protect assets from creditors. But creditors have protections, too.

For example, a transfer to an offshore trust cannot be a fraudulent conveyance. In 1571, the Statute of Elizabeth declared void all transfers of property made with the intent of defrauding creditors. The U.S. and many other countries have similar statutes. The offshore trust must be established under the laws of a foreign country that recognizes trusts but that isn't overly bothered by the Statute of Elizabeth. Currently these countries are Gibraltar, the Cayman Islands, the Bahamas, the Cook Islands, and Cyprus.

Nonetheless, the grantor should also be concerned with the fraudulent conveyance laws here at home. Some grantors smugly assume that any U.S. judgment against them based on a fraudulent conveyance will be unenforceable in the foreign country of their trust. This may be, but assets such as the family residence remaining in the U.S. are still subject to creditors' claims. Moreover, the grantor might be subject to criminal penalties.

Offshore trusts also create problems for the attorney. For whom do you think the creditors will chase when they discover that the grantor's assets have all gone on an island vacation? Perhaps the solution is that no attorney should draft an offshore trust who doesn't have one of his or her own.

Offshore trusts tend to be expensive. They cost approximately $15,000 to set up and $5,000 per year thereafter.

On balance, offshore trusts raise significant legal, financial, and ethical questions. For a few the offshore trust may be a panacea; but for the rest of us it will remain a dream.

In the next chapter we will look at some less exotic, more traditional ways of keeping creditors at bay.

CHAPTER 22

Protecting Your Booty

When we last saw the Artful Dodger, he was in a state of acute paranoia over the prospect of hordes of creditors swooping down to plunder his precious possessions. (This is highly unlikely since Art is the type of person who rushes down to pay his monthly utility bill in person and has receipts to prove it going back to the Great Depression.) Having reluctantly decided to pass on the offshore trust, Art is casting about for more conventional ways to preserve wealth. So he dropped by his clever attorney's office to have a chat.

EXEMPT ASSETS: First off, under state law even the most rapacious creditor cannot grab certain assets. For example, Art, having reached the age of 65, finds that he and Ellie have a homestead exemption of $100,000. This means that up to $100,000 of equity in the family residence is secure. (Art's son, Roger, and his wife, because neither is 65, have an exemption of $75,000.)

Other exempt assets, to name a few, are automobiles (up to $1,200 in value), household furnishings and personal effects, jewelry and works of art (up to $2,500 in value), life insurance policies (up to $4,000 of the loan value), and certain retirement benefits.

Although state exemptions are nice to have around, they are so limited as to provide little comfort to most of us.

LIVING TRUSTS: Forget living trusts as a means of protecting assets. At best, a living trust may slow, but will not stop the onslaught of creditors.

TAX-SAVING TRUSTS: Perhaps you recall the various tax-saving trusts Art can set up for Ellie: the bypass trust that escapes tax in Ellie's estate, and the QTIP trust that qualifies for the marital deduction (or the QDOT trust, if the surviving spouse is not a U.S. citizen).

Each of these trusts, if properly drafted, contains a spendthrift provision. This provision states that the trust is exempt from the claims of the beneficiary's creditors. Thus, Art can place assets in trust for the benefit of Ellie that will be secure. Creditors can only look long-ingly at these trust assets, much as Aesop's fox looked at the hanging grapes.

CHARITABLE TRUSTS: In chapters 15 we discussed the tax advantages of Art's creating a charitable remainder trust. A charitable remainder trust also gives Art protection against creditors. The assets in the hands of the charity cannot be touched. Art's creditors can, however, reach trust distributions after Art has received them. If Art doesn't like the idea of creditors swooping down on these distributions, he can instruct the trustee to invest solely in growth stock. Then there will be no distributions upon which to swoop. And Art can delay receiving further distribution until his financial troubles have blown over.

All of this makes Art feel somewhat more secure. But at night, on his headboard, the black crows of worry still roost. Perhaps in the next chapter we can put a few more of these birds to flight.

CHAPTER 23

Protecting
More of Your Booty

Recently, the Artful Dodger's spirits have been on the rise. He now knows creditors can't reach the money he will receive from his charitable trust. Moreover, at his death the property he leaves in trust to his wife, Ellie, also will be protected. To the annoyance of everyone around him, Art has taken to singing, under his breath, over and over again, "Oh, No, They Can't Take That Away From Me." Eager to learn more about asset protection, Art wandered back into his clever attorney's office to find out more about protecting his booty.

GENERATION-SKIPPING TRUSTS: In estate planning, Art can do for his son, Roger, what Art cannot do for himself. For example, Art cannot protect his property from his creditors' claims merely by creating a living trust. Art can, however, give Roger property in trust either during Art's life or at death. If the trust contains a spendthrift clause, the property will be outside the reach of Roger's creditors. Moreover this trust can continue on for the benefit of the little Dodgers after Roger's death.

As we discussed chapter 5, the primary purpose of such a trust is to pass Art's property to his grandchildren (Roger's children) without its being taxed in Roger's estate. That the property can pass free of creditors' claims as well is an added bonus.

Art must bear in mind that once the assets of a trust are distributed to a beneficiary, they are no longer protected. Art may decide, therefore, to put a "sprinkling power" in his trust. This allows the trustee to choose to which of Art's family members to make distributions. Thus, the trustee can choose *not* to make distributions to a child or grandchild whose creditors are camped out on the welcome mat.

GIFTS TO SPOUSE: Years ago Art, quite foolishly, became a general partner with his son, Roger, in one of Roger's ill-begotten schemes to get rich quick. Though nothing bad has happened yet, Art feels it is only a matter of time before Roger's idiot scheme puts him at personal risk. Art has heard of people, especially professionals, giving their property to a spouse to avoid the claims of potential creditors.

Does this scheme work? Possibly. As we have seen, Art can give Ellie any amount, tax free. But the gift must not be a fraud on creditors. Also the gift must be irrevocable and cannot be a mere sham. In other words, no crossed-fingers-behind-the-back stuff.

There is one obvious problem. If Ellie ever gets really fed up with Art (and who could blame her?) and divorces him, Ellie gets to keep all the property. And all Art will end up with is Medi-Cal eligibility.

Transfers of life insurance involve less risk to Art. He can transfer the ownership of life insurance, naming Ellie as the beneficiary, to her, thereby placing both the policy and its proceeds beyond the reach of Art's creditors. If Art and Ellie do part company, all Art will have lost is the cash surrender value of the policy.

CORPORATIONS AND PARTNERSHIPS: Always eager to make more money, Art, in his spare time, has invented a fully biodegradable beer can. Art worries about the liability he might incur if his invention doesn't work out just right. (Several cans, for example, have biodegraded prematurely, leaving a mess in Ellie's refrigerator.)

By incorporating his venture Art can probably limit his liability to the assets of the corporation. A corporation can be fairly simple. In fact, Art can act as sole shareholder, director, and officer.

An alternative to a corporation is the limited liability company (LLC) which became available in California in 1994. The LLC is taxed like a partnership (which is simpler than a corporation), yet it affords the same protection from liability as a corporation.

INSURING AGAINST THE RISK: Many of the most serious risks Art faces, such as those involving personal injury or property damage, are covered by insurance Art has purchased on his home, car, and business. Of course, Art should periodically review these policies to make sure he is adequately protected. He should also consider buying an umbrella policy, which increases the protection afforded by all these policies. Since an umbrella policy only supplements existing insurance, it is surprisingly affordable.

In the next chapter we will explore the question, "Do you need a conservatorship?" Hint: If you think you do, you probably don't.

CHAPTER 24

If You Think You Do, You Probably Don't

One day the Artful Dodger and his wife, Ellie, dropped in on their clever attorney to discuss estate planning. While Art was out wiping the chalk mark off the tire of his Geo Metro, Ellie told the clever attorney about something that had been bothering her. At least once a day, Ellie confided, she walks into a room to get something and ends up standing in the middle of the room without any idea why she is there. "Perhaps I should know something about conservatorships," Ellie said, smiling weakly.

Two thoughts popped into the clever attorney's head. The first thought he disclosed to Ellie. It was that people who think they may need a conservatorship, generally don't; and people who don't, often do.

The second thought he kept to himself. It was that he had the same problem as Ellie. Only it happened to him several times each day.

Even though not a candidate for a conservatorship, Ellie wanted to know more about it.

A conservatorship is a court proceeding to take care of people who cannot take care of themselves or who might fall prey to the undue influence of others. A person does *not* have to be incompetent to have a conservatorship. In fact, a person who is competent can petition for the appointment of a conservator for himself or herself.

First, let's get the nomenclature out of the way. The person under a disability is the conservatee. The person charged with the responsibility of caring for the conservatee is the conservator. (As you Gilbert and Sullivan fans know, in the case of a minor the parties are known as the ward and the guardian, respectively.)

The conservator of the estate manages the conservatee's property. The conservator of the person manages the conservatee's personal care.

The court proceeding is started when a petition for the appointment of a conservator is filed by an interested party. Unless the petition is filed by the proposed conservatee, the proposed conservatee must be served with a citation advising him or her of the petition and the hearing date and ordering him or her to attend.

Our judicial system zealously protects the rights of incapacitated people, so much so that some judges have their own investigators to independently apprise them of a conservatee's situation. After the petition is filed, the court investigator interviews the proposed conservatee and files a comprehensive report describing the conservatee's condition. The investigator asks the conservatee if he or she wants the conservatorship and if he or she approves of the proposed conservator. The investigator also makes recommendations as to the need for the conservatorship and the appropriate level of care.

Unless unwilling or physically unable, the proposed conservatee attends the hearing. The judge may question the proposed conservator and conservatee to satisfy himself or herself that the appointment is appropriate. If the proposed conservatee objects to being conserved, the court appoints an attorney to represent his or her interests and sets the matter for further hearing. If the proposed conservatee makes no objection and the court finds it is in his or her best interests, a conservator is appointed and letters of conservatorship issue. These letters give the conservator authority to act on the conservatee's behalf.

In the next chapter we will see how conservatorships can be used to do some crucial estate planning for individuals who, due to their incapacity, can't do it themselves.

CHAPTER 25

Doing for Others . . .

When we wound up the last chapter, the conservator had just been appointed and letters of conservatorship had issued.

THE BOND: Unless the conservatee is competent and waives it, the court will require the conservator to post a bond. The amount of the bond is equal to the value of the personal property of the estate plus the estimated annual income earned by those assets. For example, if the conservatorship assets (exclusive of real property) total $500,000, the bond will be set at $525,000, assuming an annual income of 5%. The cost of this bond can range from $600 to $1,200 per year.

Think of a bond as an insurance policy that protects the conservatorship estate from loss if the conservator goes "over the hill" with the conservatorship assets. The amount of the bond can be reduced to the extent assets are deposited in a blocked bank account and receipts are filed with the court.

THE INVENTORY AND APPRAISEMENT: The conscientious reader of this book will no doubt have noticed the similarity between conservatorship and probate proceedings. (The rest of you really should pay closer attention.) As in the case of probate, the conservator files an inventory with the court listing all conservatorship assets. The assets are valued by a court-appointed referee.

COURT REPORTS: After the first year and thereafter every two years, the conservator files with the court a report that must include a balanced accounting.

The conservator is entitled to a fee that the judge must approve. This fee is usually based on the hours spent handling the conservatorship. Judges are scrutinous of these fees and seldom allow them in excess of $3/4$ of 1% of the gross estate per year, which for an estate of $500,000 is $3,750. If the conservator is a family member, the fee often is waived.

Some actions of the conservator, such as selling the conservatee's residence, require advance court approval. Before deciding the matter, the judge may order the court investigator to visit the conservatee and advise the judge of the conservatee's wishes and ability to remain in the residence.

IT'S NEVER TOO LATE: A conservator can even petition the court to do estate planning for the conservatee. By this procedure, the court and the conservator can accomplish some of those things the conservatee probably would want to do himself or herself.

Take the case of the Artful Dodger's Aunt Dottie, who is mentally incompetent. Aunt Dottie never got around to doing much in the way of estate planning. Now she lacks the capacity to write a will, create a trust, or make gifts. As a result, unless something is done, unnecessary estate taxes and administration expenses will be incurred at her death.

In times past, Aunt Dottie's conservator could do little more than wring his or her hands. Today, however, the conservator can petition the court to do many of the things Aunt Dottie could have done were she competent.

For example, Aunt Dottie was in the habit of giving her children annual gifts of $10,000. Aunt Dottie's conservator can seek court approval to continue making the gifts on her behalf, thus reducing the size of her taxable estate.

The court can also authorize the conservator to set up a living trust for Aunt Dottie to avoid probate or to change Aunt Dottie's estate plan so as to save estate taxes.

An alternative to the conservatorship is the living trust which many find attractive because it usually requires no court involvement. One important limitation of the living trust, however, is that the trustee is not permitted to do estate planning for someone like Aunt Dottie.

In the next chapter we will meet Uncle Albert—looking absolutely dreadful.

CHAPTER 26

Understanding Medi-Cal

Every family, it seems, has one, and the Dodger family is no exception. Art's Uncle Albert is the rogue bachelor of the family who over the years has lived the good life while making and losing fortunes in exotic foreign ventures. Uncle Al drops in every so often to see the Dodger family and, incidentally, to borrow a couple thousand dollars to tide him over to his next fortune.

Art was reminded of Uncle Al just the other day—rather vividly, in fact—when he opened the front door and found Uncle Al standing on the stoop looking absolutely dreadful. It seems Al's diet of martinis and bar snacks has caught up with him. His liver has finally gone out on strike. His doctor says he needs nursing home care.

Of course, this medical emergency has caught Uncle Al in one of his financial troughs. He is, therefore, more than merely curious to know what public benefits are available to cover the cost of his care.

THE COST OF CARE: Nursing home care in California costs an average of $2,900 per month. It can run as high as $3,500 a month, with locked facilities costing even more.

MEDICARE: Medicare is a federal program run as part of the Social Security system. It provides no benefits for mere "custodial care." It does provide limited support for "skilled care" but only after a minimum of three days hospitalization. Medicare then pays all the cost of the first 20 days in a nursing home, everything over $84.50 per day for the next 80 days, and nothing after that. Supplemental Medicare insurance pays only the $84.50 for days 21 through 100. Since Uncle Al's liver cannot even be brought to the bargaining table in 100 days, Al must look elsewhere for help.

MEDI-CAL: Medi-Cal is a combined federal and state program designed to provide nursing home benefits for the needy. Medi-Cal defines need on the basis of income and assets. Al, while in the nursing home, must first spend all his own income on the cost of his care (less only $35 per month) before Medi-Cal will spend a dime.

Al is also limited in what he can own. For example, he can have no more than $2,000 of nonexempt assets. The most important exempt asset is his residence. Remarkably, the value of the residence doesn't matter. Al could reside in the Hearst Castle (which, unfortunately, he doesn't) and still qualify for Medi-Cal benefits. As long as he declares his intent to return home, his residence will remain exempt regardless of the gravity of his medical condition.

Also exempt are the following assets:

- The family farm or business, regardless of value.
- Rental property with an equity not exceeding $6,000. (Thanks, a lot.)
- Equipment and materials used in a person's employment.
- Other miscellaneous assets including a burial plot, a car, home furnishings, personal effects, and certain life insurance.

Some assets, like IRAs, work-related pensions, and annuities, although not exempt, do not affect Medi-Cal eligibility. This is true, however, only if the individual is receiving regular distributions, which, of course, Medi-Cal claps onto.

In the following chapter we will look at strategies calculated to preserve wealth while still qualifying for Medi-Cal.

CHAPTER 27

Some Medi-Cal Strategies

When we last looked in on Uncle Albert, he was laid up in a nursing home, wondering how he could qualify for Medi-Cal without completely beggaring himself. The Artful Dodger's clever attorney dropped in to discuss some strategies that might help Al qualify for Medi-Cal while hanging onto at least some of the remnants of his last fortune.

SPENDING DOWN: Before Al can qualify for Medi-Cal, he must spend down to $2,000 in assets that are not exempt. During Al's drinking days, this would have been a happy prospect. Now, instead of worldly pleasures Al should spend his money on health care, home repairs, clothing, an automobile, home furnishings, personal debts, and, most importantly, the satisfaction of his home mortgage. Obviously, the trick is to spend money to reduce debt or on exempt assets.

GIVING IT AWAY: It occurs to Al that, rather than spend all his money, he should give it (wink, wink) to his nephew, Art. Then if he ever gets back on his feet again, Art can transfer the money back to him and all will be as before. This approach presents several problems.

First, Medi-Cal will delay Al's eligibility if he gives property away within 36 months of his applying for benefits.

Second, any transfer to Art with the understanding that Al can get the money back is fraudulent. And actually *getting* the money back may prove tricky.

Gifts of money or other nonexempt property can be an effective planning tool if you can wait three years to apply for Medi-Cal. This is especially true if the gift is to a child, for example, who would have inherited the property anyway.

In fact, sometimes it makes sense to give away your residence even though this asset does not affect your Medi-Cal eligibility. In some cases (especially if you are not married), Medi-Cal is entitled to a lien on your residence equal to the cost of your nursing home care. Although this lien is not enforceable until you die (or sell your residence), it will reduce the value of your children's inheritance.

Al has a great idea. He will put his residence into a living trust. Since he will not own the residence at his death, he reasons, it will escape the Medi-Cal lien. No soap. Medi-Cal can enforce its lien against a residence even if it is held in a living trust.

DIVORCE: The thought of a couple, married over 50 years, divorcing solely to protect the resources of the well spouse is draconian. It is also an unfortunate fact of life in Medi-Cal planning. For the assets of *both* spouses, community and separate, are counted in determining Medi-Cal eligibility for long-term care. Medi-Cal allows the well spouse, with certain exceptions, to keep non exempt assets worth only $74,820 (1995 amount, indexed upward annually). Therefore, to avoid depleting the estates of both spouses, divorce becomes a pragmatic option.

Uncle Albert advised the clever attorney that he had no qualms whatsoever about divorce if it would accelerate his eligibility, and that he would certainly consider it if he ever got married.

INCOME: The well spouse can keep all his or her own income but no more than $1,871 per month (1995 amount, indexed upward annually) of the sick spouse's income for living expenses. To determine whose income it is, Medi-Cal looks only at the name on the check. For example, if the sick spouse's retirement check can be issued in the well spouse's name, the well spouse can keep the entire proceeds. (I never promised that Medi-Cal rules made any sense.)

In the next chapter you will get an entirely biased view of how to pick your own clever attorney.

CHAPTER 28

Choosing Your Own Clever Attorney

Now that you know something about estate planning, you just might want to find your own clever attorney to put some of these concepts to work for you. Here are some thoughts on how you might go about this.

REFERRALS: There is no better way to choose an attorney than to profit from someone else's experience. Ask around among your friends, your accountant, your banker, your analyst. Chances are, before long, the names of one or two attorneys will come up over and over again.

If you have had a good experience with an attorney in the past (I know what you're thinking), the obvious place to start is with him or her. Be sure to ask if estate planning is one of his or her specialties. If not, this attorney probably knows the territory and can refer you to someone locally who is well regarded professionally.

ADVERTISING: I must warn you that what follows is an entirely biased opinion on the subject of legal advertising: When it comes to choosing an attorney from the yellow pages, my advice is, "Let your fingers take a rest." It is simply not true that the size of an ad is inversely proportional to the competency of the attorney. But neither is it any guaranty that the attorney who placed the ad is well qualified. You should no more pick your attorney on the basis of advertising than you would your family doctor.

At one time attorneys were ethically forbidden to advertise. Now, the floodgates are open, and tasteless, sometimes downright misleading ads abound, not only in the yellow pages but throughout the media as well. When an attorney tells you how wonderful he or she is in bold face type, take it with a grain of salt.

The yellow pages *can* serve one useful purpose. At the end of all that advertising, you will find an "Attorney Guide" listing lawyers who hold themselves out as practicing in various fields. For an estate planning attorney, look under "Wills, Trusts, and Estate Planning." This guide at least tells you the attorney's own characterization of his or her area of expertise.

CERTIFICATION: The State Bar of California certifies attorneys who have demonstrated proficiency in certain fields. Probate, Estate Planning and Trusts is one such field. Taxation is another. To become a specialist, an attorney must pass an examination in his or her chosen specialty and then demonstrate both experience and special training in that field. California, as of 1995, has 525 specialists in Probate, Estate Planning and Trusts and 478 specialists in Taxation.

Although some competent estate planners are not certified in either of these fields, certification is at least one factor to weigh in your decision.

PEER REVIEW: A national directory of lawyers (known as the Martindale-Hubbell Law Directory) is available at most public libraries. Here you can find out, among other things, where an attorney went to school, when he or she was graduated, the type of clientele he or she represents, and the area of his or her practice.

More importantly, you will see how fellow attorneys rate both an attorney's ethics and competency. Martindale-Hubbell goes to great lengths to obtain a fair consensus of an attorney's reputation among his or her peers. As a result, attorneys often rely on these ratings when making referrals. Don't overlook this valuable source of information.

Now that you have found your own clever attorney, let's see how you can assist in preparing the estate plan that's right for you—and for the right price.

CHAPTER 29

Preparing for Your Own Clever Attorney

Years ago, Art learned in high school physics that there are certain immutable laws of cause and effect. To his dismay, the same immutable laws apply every time he ventures into his clever attorney's office to discuss his estate plan. For the predictable effect of each visit is a bill. Here are some suggestions that will reduce the time (not to mention the bill) you (and Art) would otherwise spend with your attorney developing your estate plan.

THE FACTS: Most estate planning attorneys have clients fill out a questionnaire listing assets and liabilities. If possible, get a copy of this questionnaire, fill it out, and drop it off at your attorney's office *before* your first conference.

If your attorney doesn't have a questionnaire, make up your own financial statement. Better yet, if you have your personal finances on a computer, run off a statement of assets and liabilities. Don't forget to list all retirement plans along with life insurance policies.

You should also prepare a list of the names and addresses of members of your immediate family, in addition to those persons you named in your will (or trust) as beneficiaries or executors (trustees). In large families it is helpful to diagram your family tree, showing the relationships of your nearest relatives. And don't forget relatives who have died leaving children.

Even if you are not giving a farthing to your relatives, your attorney will need this information. At your death, the law requires that your heirs be notified even if you disinherited them. This is not out of a misguided sense of fun but rather to give all interested parties notice of a probate proceeding in case they wish to contest it. (Appendix H and I are sample Confidential Client Questionnaires, containing financial and family information, respectively, that you may find useful.)

THE DOCUMENTS: Your attorney will want to review certain documents that are important in preparing your estate plan. Don't forget to bring copies of the following to your first meeting:

- Deeds to real property. If you can't find a deed, the local title company will obtain a copy, usually at no charge, if you provide the assessor's parcel number.
- Life insurance policies, with all change of beneficiary forms.
- Buy-sell, partnership, and other agreements relating to any business you own.
- Beneficiary designation statements for all retirement assets (like IRAs and Keogh plans).
- Your existing estate planning documents.

BONING UP: Estate planning has become very complex. Your attorney must try to explain, in a short time, complicated estate planning concepts that took him several semesters in law school to master.

Moreover, the attorney who can communicate in plain English has yet to be born. It is no wonder, therefore, that most clients' eyes start to glaze over three minutes into a discussion on QTIP trusts.

The more you already know about the general concepts of estate planning, the better you will understand what your attorney is trying to tell you. And the less time he or she will spend in explanation. It is well worth your time, therefore, to spend a few hours boning up in advance. This knowledge is not hard to come by.

Every bookstore has a legal section with shelves groaning under the weight of estate planning books written for the nonlawyer. I shamelessly hasten to add that this little book is not a bad place to start. And to reward those of you who have stuck it out this far, I have included crib notes for you (Appendix J), summarizing some of the techniques we have discussed. Feel free to take them with you when you next visit your clever attorney.

By following these suggestions you will enter your attorney's office prepared to help him or her help you. And you will have a far better chance of ending up with the right estate plan for the right price.

In the next chapter we will look as some questions you might just want to discuss with your clever attorney.

CHAPTER 30

Questions to Ask
Your Own Clever Attorney

Nobody, not even the Artful Dodger's clever attorney, is perfect. In fact, just the other day Art's clever attorney discovered he had screwed up.

WHO SHOULD PAY ESTATE TAXES? For years Art's Aunt Agatha has lived in a Carmel cottage Art and Ellie own. Since Agatha is as poor as a church mouse, Art and Ellie have willed the cottage to her so that, if she survives them, she will always have a place to live. The Dodgers' wills did not state on whom the burden of estate taxes would fall. As a result, under California law taxes would be prorated among all beneficiaries, and poor Aunt Agatha would have to sell the cottage to pay her share.

Fortunately, this problem was discovered by the clever attorney during a routine review of the Dodgers' estate file. Before his second cup of coffee, he was on the phone to the Dodgers suggesting their wills be changed so the cottage will pass to Agatha free of tax.

The point is simple: Be sure to discuss with your attorney just where you want the burden of taxes to fall.

Estate planning requires detailed fact gathering. Even the cleverest attorney, on occasion, fails to ask questions, such as this one, that are crucial to an estate plan. Here are some other occasionally overlooked questions you just might want to discuss with your clever attorney:

WHAT IF MY CHILD DIES FIRST? Art and Ellie have willed most of their estate to their son, Roger. If Roger dies before they do, their estate passes to Roger's children. The Dodgers' wills read this way because that is the way the standard will in their clever attorney's word processor reads. But what of Roger's widow? The vision of the little Dodgers sitting around the table eating smoked salmon while their mother eats canned tuna is disturbing.

Art and Ellie may just want to give some of their estate to Roger's widow, who, after all, will have the responsibility of raising their grandchildren.

HOW SHOULD I DISPOSE OF FAMILY HEIRLOOMS? If Art and Ellie had more than one child, they like most folks would probably leave their family heirlooms, memorabilia, jewelry, and the like to their children equally. This often sows the seeds of future sibling warfare. ("Mother always wanted *me* to have Aunt Mildred's milking stool.") It is usually not practical to list heirlooms item by item in your will. Ask your attorney about other ways to distribute these assets. For example, you can tag heirlooms with the children's initials. Or attach a letter with specific instructions to your will. Or, if the kids can't agree, designate just how the property can be divided by lot and designate someone outside the family (who, incidentally, will never forgive you) to preside over the division.

SHOULD I GIVE MY SPOUSE THE RIGHT TO DECIDE WHO WILL INHERIT MY ESTATE? If Art wills his property to Ellie, in trust, he must state what will happen to the property on Ellie's death. Instead of having the estate pass to Roger, Art can give Ellie the right, during her lifetime, to choose how Art's estate ultimately will be distributed among Roger and the little Dodgers. This is called a limited power of appointment.

If Roger doesn't need any more money, Ellie could leave Art's estate to Roger's children instead. And Ellie could choose which of her grandchildren should inherit. For example, she could leave a healthy amount to the grandchild who is selflessly teaching handicapped children and little or nothing to the grandchild who dropped out of school at 14 to express himself on a Harley-Davidson.

For the finale, I have chosen to reveal the legal equivalent of the secret of the universe when it comes to saving taxes.

CHAPTER 31

The Ultimate Tax Dodge

For purely theatrical reasons, I have saved the best part for last. Here now is the Godzilla of all tax loopholes.

Let's say you are a single person with $1,000,000. You want to take a cruise around the world in the hopes of meeting a single person with $2,000,000 dollars. Want to know how to charge at least 37% of your trip on Uncle Sam's master card? The answer is simple—take the cruise. Or as the Nike people say, "Just do it."

In Ben Franklin's day, a penny saved was a penny earned. That was before estate taxes. Today it is more accurate to say, a penny saved is a penny taxed.

In all of our Byzantine tax planning we often overlook the fact that consumption is the ultimate tax dodge. Uncle Sam cannot tax it if it isn't there. The virtues we were taught as children—prudence, moderation, thrift—serve us less well as we get older (At least from the stand point of estate planning).

You all remember Aesop's fable about the ant and the grasshopper. The ant worked 16 hour days gathering food for the winter. The grasshopper, on the other hand, danced and drank and regaled all his friends with tasteless lawyer jokes. What Aesop didn't tell you was that when the ant died (probably from stress), Uncle Sam made a killing. But when the grasshopper died (probably from a failed liver), Uncle Sam got nothing.

People are either ants or grasshoppers. If you are reading this chapter, you are an ant. The grasshoppers, having no money to worry about, lost interest in this book a long time ago.

The problem with you ants is that you can't stop being ants—even when your storerooms are bursting. But you must try.

And, if you are interested, there is an even more advantageous way to spend your money. Why not consider spending it on charity? A charitable gift gives you a double bonus. Not only does the gift escape taxation in your estate, but you also get to deduct it from your current income. If you are in a 37% income tax bracket (both state and federal) and a 50% estate tax bracket, a gift of $1,000 to your favorite charity will cost you only $315. And when you make a gift to charity during your lifetime, you will get the recognition you deserve, now rather than after you are gone.

So whether your consumption takes the form of doing things that give you pleasure or giving money to charity (which also may give you pleasure), Uncle Sam is picking up some of the tab.

One last thought. It is the shared ambition of most of us to reduce our taxes. But we must not forget that a government's ability to tax is at the very base of its ability to survive.

I admit that Uncle Sam's profligacy with our tax dollars at times suggests the need for a conservatorship. He has, however, given us the type of government that has allowed us to accumulate our booty in the first place. So, in the end, perhaps there are worse things you could do than pay some taxes. The Artful Dodger, or course, doesn't agree with this. But Art, as we know, is an especially tough nut.

This is the last chapter because I have pretty much run out of things to say. (It is simply *not* true that I ran out in chapter 12.) I have enjoyed writing this little book. I hope it helps you develop with the advice of your own clever attorney, an estate plan that is right for you. At least, now at cocktail parties, you can let drop mention of QTIPs, QPRTs, or QDOTs with the nonchalance of someone who really knows.

On behalf of myself and the entire Dodger clan, I thank you for your readership.

1. WASTING ART'S EXEMPTION

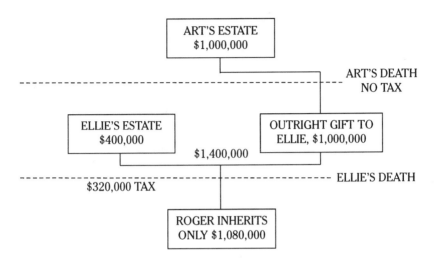

ART'S ESTATE
$1,000,000

ART'S DEATH
NO TAX

ELLIE'S ESTATE
$400,000

OUTRIGHT GIFT TO
ELLIE, $1,000,000

$1,400,000

$320,000 TAX

ELLIE'S DEATH

ROGER INHERITS
ONLY $1,080,000

2. GETTING TWO EXEMPTIONS FOR THE PRICE OF ONE

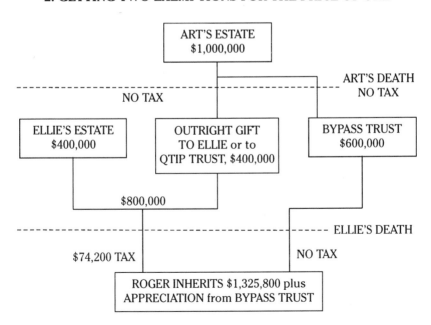

ART'S ESTATE
$1,000,000

ART'S DEATH
NO TAX

NO TAX

ELLIE'S ESTATE
$400,000

OUTRIGHT GIFT
TO ELLIE or to
QTIP TRUST, $400,000

BYPASS TRUST
$600,000

$800,000

ELLIE'S DEATH

$74,200 TAX

NO TAX

ROGER INHERITS $1,325,800 plus
APPRECIATION from BYPASS TRUST

THE GENERATION-SKIPPING TRUST

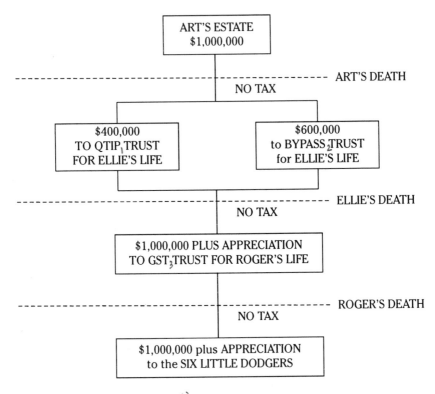

ART'S ESTATE
$1,000,000

- ART'S DEATH
NO TAX

| $400,000 TO QTIP TRUST FOR ELLIE'S LIFE | $600,000 to BYPASS TRUST for ELLIE'S LIFE |

- ELLIE'S DEATH
NO TAX

$1,000,000 PLUS APPRECIATION
TO GST TRUST FOR ROGER'S LIFE

- ROGER'S DEATH
NO TAX

$1,000,000 plus APPRECIATION
to the SIX LITTLE DODGERS

(1,2,3)
Can assets in trust be traded (bought & sold) - or
must original asset be maintained forever?

DURABLE POWER OF ATTORNEY FOR HEALTH CARE
WARNING TO PERSON EXECUTING THIS DOCUMENT

THIS IS AN IMPORTANT LEGAL DOCUMENT THAT IS AUTHORIZED BY THE KEENE HEALTH CARE AGENT ACT. BEFORE EXECUTING THIS DOCUMENT, YOU SHOULD KNOW THESE IMPORTANT FACTS:

1. This document gives the person you designate as your agent (the attorney-in-fact) the power to make health care decisions for you. Your agent must act consistently with your desires as stated in this document or otherwise made known.

2. Except as you otherwise specify in this document, this document gives your agent the power to consent to your doctor's not giving treatment or stopping treatment necessary to keep you alive.

3. Notwithstanding this document, you have the right to make medical and other health care decisions for yourself as long as you can give informed consent with respect to the particular decision. In addition, no treatment may be given to you over your objection at the time, and health care necessary to keep you alive may not be stopped or withheld if you object at the time.

4. This document gives your agent authority to consent, to refuse to consent, or to withdraw consent to any care, treatment, service, or procedure to maintain, diagnose, or treat a physical or mental condition. This power is subject to any statement of your desires and any limitations that you include in this document. You may state in this document any types of treatment that you do not desire. In addition, a court can take away the power of your agent to make health care decisions for you if your agent (1) authorizes anything that is illegal; (2) acts contrary to your known desires; or (3) where your desires are not known, does anything that is clearly contrary to your best interests.

5. Unless you specify a shorter period in this document, this power will exist for an indefinite period of time.

6. You have the right to revoke the authority of your agent by notifying your agent or your treating doctor, hospital, or other health care provider orally or in writing of your revocation.

7. Your agent has the right to examine your medical records and to consent to their disclosure unless you limit this right in this document.

8. Unless you otherwise specify in this document, this document gives your agent the power after you die to authorize an autopsy, donate your body or parts thereof for transplant or therapeutic or educational or scientific purposes, and direct the disposition of your remains.

9. This document revokes any prior durable power of attorney for health care.

10. You should carefully read and follow the witnessing procedure described at the end of this form. This document will not be valid unless you comply with the witnessing procedure.

11. If there is anything in this document that you do not understand, you should ask a lawyer to explain it to you.

12. Your agent may need this document immediately in case of an emergency that requires a decision concerning your health care. Either keep this document where it is immediately available to your agent and alternate agents or give each of them an executed copy of this document. You may also want to give your doctor(s) an executed copy of this document.

13. Do not use this form if you are a conservatee under the Lanterman-Petris-Short Act and you want to appoint your conservator as your agent. You can do that only if the appointment document includes a certificate of your attorney.

1. DESIGNATION OF HEALTH CARE AGENT:

I, _____, do hereby designate and appoint _____ as my attorney-in-fact to make health care decisions for me as authorized in this document. For the purposes of this document, "health care decisions" means consent, refusal of consent, or withdrawal of consent to any care, treatment, service, or procedure to maintain, diagnose, or treat an individual's physical or mental condition.

2. CREATION OF DURABLE POWER OF ATTORNEY FOR HEALTH CARE:

By this document I intend to create a durable power of attorney for health care under Sections 2430 to 2443, inclusive, of the California Civil Code. This power of attorney is authorized by the Keene Health Care Agent Act and shall be construed in accordance with the provisions of Sections 2400 to 2506, inclusive, of the California Civil Code. This power of attorney shall not be affected by my subsequent incapacity.

3. GENERAL STATEMENT OF AUTHORITY GRANTED:

Subject to any limitations in this document, I hereby grant to my agent full power and authority to make health care decisions for me to the same extent that I could make such decisions for myself if I had the capacity to do so. In exercising this authority, my agent shall make health care decisions that are consistent with my desires as stated in this document or otherwise made known to my agent, including, but not limited to, my desires concerning obtaining or refusing or withdrawing life-prolonging care, treatment, services, and procedures.

4. DESIRES, SPECIAL PROVISIONS, AND LIMITATIONS:

[Your agent must make health care decisions that are consistent with your known desires. You can, but are not required to, state your desires in the space provided below. You should consider whether you want to include a statement of your desires concerning decisions to withhold or remove life-sustaining treatment. For your convenience, some general statements concerning the withholding and removal of life-sustaining treatment are set out below. If you agree with one of these statements, you may *initial* that statement. READ ALL OF THESE STATEMENTS CAREFULLY BEFORE YOU SELECT ONE TO INITIAL. You can also write your own statement concerning life-sustaining treatment and/or other matters relating to your health care. BY LAW, YOUR AGENT IS NOT PERMITTED TO CONSENT ON YOUR BEHALF TO ANY OF THE FOLLOWING: COMMITMENT TO OR PLACEMENT IN A MENTAL HEALTH TREATMENT FACILITY, CONVULSIVE TREATMENT, PSYCHO-SURGERY, STERILIZATION, OR ABORTION. In every other respect, your agent may make health care decisions for you to the same extent you could make them for yourself if you were capable of doing so. If you want to limit in any other way the authority given your agent by this document, you should state the limits in the space below. If you do not initial one of the printed statements or write your own statement, your agent will have the broad powers to make health care decisions on your behalf that are set forth herein, except to the extent that there are limits provided by law.]

> I do not want my life to be prolonged and I do not want life-sustaining treatment to be provided or continued if the burdens of the treatment outweigh the expected benefits. I want my agent to consider the relief of suffering and the quality as well as the extent of the possible extension of my life in making decisions concerning life-sustaining treatment.

If this statement reflects your desires, initial here._____

> I want my life to be prolonged and I want life-sustaining treatment to be provided unless I am in a coma that my doctors reasonably believe to be irreversible. Once my doctors have reasonably concluded I am in an irreversible coma, I do not want life-sustaining treatment to be provided or continued.

If this statement reflects your desires, initial here._____

> I want my life to be prolonged to the greatest extent possible without regard to my condition, the chances I have for recovery, or the cost of the procedures.

If this statement reflects your desires, initial here._____

> Other or additional statements of desires, special provisions, or limitations

_____

_____

5. INSPECTION AND DISCLOSURE OF INFORMATION RELATING TO MY PHYSICAL OR MENTAL HEALTH:

Subject to any limitations set forth elsewhere in this document, my agent shall have the power and authority to do all of the following:

A. Request, review, and receive any information, verbal or written, regarding my physical or mental health, including but not limited to medical and hospital records;

B. Execute on my behalf any releases or other documents that may be required to obtain this information;

C. Consent to the disclosure of this information.

6. SIGNING DOCUMENTS, WAIVERS, AND RELEASES:

Where necessary to implement the health care decisions that my agent is authorized by this document to make, my agent has the power and authority to execute on my behalf all of the following:

A. Documents titled or purporting to be a "Refusal to Permit Treatment" and "Leaving Hospital Against Medical Advice."

B. Any necessary waiver or release from liability required by a hospital or physician.

7. AUTOPSY; ANATOMICAL GIFTS; DISPOSITION OF REMAINS:

Subject to any limitations in this document, my agent has the power and authority to do all of the following:

A. Authorize an autopsy under Health and Safety Code Section 7113.

B. Make a disposition of a part or parts of my body under the Uniform Anatomical Gifts Act.

C. Direct the disposition of my remains under Health and Safety Code Section 7100.

8. DURATION:

This power of attorney will exist for an indefinite period of time unless otherwise specified in this document.

9. DESIGNATION OF ALTERNATE AGENTS:

If the person designated as my agent hereinabove is not available or becomes ineligible to act as my agent to make health care decisions for me or loses the mental capacity to make health care decisions for me, or if I revoke that person's appointment or authority to act as my agent to make health care decisions for me, then I designate and appoint the following persons to serve as my agent to make health care decisions for me as authorized in this document, such persons to serve in the order listed below:

First alternative agent:
Address and telephone number:
Second alternative agent:
Address and telephone number:

10. NOMINATION OF CONSERVATOR OF PERSON:

If it becomes necessary to appoint a conservator of my person, I nominate the following individuals to serve as conservator of my person, to serve alone in the order named:

First alternative agent:
Address and telephone number:
Second alternative agent:
Address and telephone number:

11. PRIOR DESIGNATIONS REVOKED:

I revoke any prior durable power of attorney for health care.

DATE AND SIGNATURE OF PRINCIPAL:

I sign my name to this Durable Power of Attorney for Health Care on
_____, 199___, at _____, California.

_____
Principal

I declare under penalty of perjury under the laws of the State of California that _____ (hereinafter the "Principal") is personally known to me; that the Principal signed or acknowledged this Durable Power of Attorney for Health Care in my presence; that the Principal appears to be of sound mind and under no duress, fraud, or undue influence; that I am not the person appointed as attorney-in-fact by this document; and that I am not a health care provider, the operator of a community care facility, or an employee of an operator of a residential care facility for the elderly.

Signed on _____, 199___, at _____, California.

_____   _____
Witness   Address

                                 _____

_____   _____
Witness   Address

                                 _____

Furthermore, I declare under penalty of perjury under the laws of the State of California that I am not related to the Principal by blood, marriage, or adoption; and, to the best of my knowledge, that I am not entitled to any part of the estate of the Principal upon the death of the Principal by operation of law or under a will, codicil, or trust now existing or by operation of law.

Dated: _____   _____
                                 Witness

                                 _____
                                 Witness

CERTIFICATE OF LAWYER

I am an attorney authorized to practice law in the State of California, and the Principal was my client at the time this power of attorney was executed. I have advised my client concerning his or her rights in connection with this power of attorney and the applicable law and the consequences of signing or not signing this power of attorney, and my client, after being so advised, has executed this power of attorney. I certify under penalty of perjury that the foregoing is true and correct.

Dated: _____   _____
                                 Attorney

DIRECTIVE TO PHYSICIANS
[Health and Safety Code 7186.5]

I, _____, being of sound mind, willfully and voluntarily make known my desire that my life shall not be artificially prolonged under the circumstances set forth below, and I do hereby declare:

1. If at any time I should have an incurable and irreversible condition that has been diagnosed by two (2) physicians and that will result in my death within a relatively short time without the administration of life-sustaining treatment or that has produced an irreversible coma or persistent vegetative state, and I am no longer able to make decisions regarding my medical treatment, I direct my attending physician, pursuant to the Natural Death Act of California, to withhold or withdraw treatment, including artificially administered nutrition and hydration, that only prolongs the process of dying or the irreversible coma or persistent vegetative state and is not necessary for my comfort or to alleviate pain.

2. If I have been diagnosed as pregnant, and that diagnosis is known to my physician, this declaration shall have no force or effect during my pregnancy.

Signed this _____ day of _____, 199___.

_____
Declarant

_____
Address

The declarant voluntarily signed this writing in my presence. I am not a health care provider, an employee of a health care provider, the operator of a community care facility, the operator of a residential care facility for the elderly, or an employee of an operator of a residential care facility for the elderly.

_____   _____
Witness   Address

The declarant voluntarily signed this writing in my presence. I am not entitled to any portion of the estate of the declarant upon his or her death under any will or codicil thereto of the declarant now existing or by operation of law. I am not a health care provider, an employee of a health care provider, the operator of a community care facility, an employee of an operator of a community care facility, the operator of a residential care facility for the elderly, or an employee of an operator of a residential care facility for the elderly

_____   _____
Witness   Address

_____   _____
Witness   Address

When recorded, return to

UNIFORM STATUTORY FORM POWER OF ATTORNEY
[California Probate Code 4401]

NOTICE: THE POWERS GRANTED BY THIS DOCUMENT ARE BROAD AND SWEEPING. THEY ARE EXPLAINED IN THE UNIFORM STATUTORY FORM POWER OF ATTORNEY ACT (CALIFORNIA PROBATE CODE SECTIONS 4400-4465). IF YOU HAVE ANY QUESTIONS ABOUT THESE POWERS, OBTAIN COMPETENT LEGAL ADVICE. THIS DOCUMENT DOES NOT AUTHORIZE ANYONE TO MAKE MEDICAL AND OTHER HEALTH CARE DECISIONS FOR YOU. YOU MAY REVOKE THIS POWER OF ATTORNEY IF YOU LATER WISH TO DO SO.

I, _____, a resident of _____, _____County, California, appoint _____, of _____, California, as my agent (attorney-in-fact) to act for me in any lawful way with respect to the following initialed subjects:

TO GRANT ALL OF THE FOLLOWING POWERS, INITIAL THE LINE IN FRONT OF (N) AND IGNORE THE LINES IN FRONT OF THE OTHER POWERS.

TO GRANT ONE OR MORE, BUT FEWER THAN ALL, OF THE FOLLOWING POWERS, INITIAL THE LINE IN FRONT OF EACH POWER YOU ARE GRANTING.

TO WITHHOLD A POWER, DO NOT INITIAL THE LINE IN FRONT OF IT. YOU MAY, BUT NEED NOT, CROSS OUT EACH POWER WITHHELD.

INITIAL

_____ (A) Real property transactions.

_____ (B) Tangible personal property transactions.

_____ (C) Stock and bond transactions.

_____ (D) Commodity and option transactions.

_____ (E) Banking and other financial institution transactions.

_____ (F) Business operating transactions.

_____ (G) Insurance and annuity transactions.

_____ (H) Estate, trust, and other beneficiary transactions.

_____ (I) Claims and litigation.

_____ (J) Personal and family maintenance.

_____ (K) Benefits from Social Security, Medicare, Medicaid, or other governmental programs, or civil or military service.

_____ (L) Retirement plan transactions.

_____ (M) Tax matters.

_____ (N) ALL OF THE POWERS LISTED ABOVE.

YOU NEED NOT INITIAL ANY OTHER LINES IF YOU INITIAL LINE (N).

SPECIAL INSTRUCTIONS

ON THE FOLLOWING LINES, YOU MAY GIVE SPECIAL INSTRUCTIONS LIMITING OR EXTENDING THE POWERS GRANTED TO YOUR AGENT.

_____

_____

_____

UNLESS YOU DIRECT OTHERWISE ABOVE, THIS POWER OF ATTORNEY IS EFFECTIVE IMMEDIATELY AND WILL CONTINUE UNTIL IT IS REVOKED.

This power of attorney will continue to be effective even though I become incapacitated.

STRIKE THE PRECEDING SENTENCE IF YOU DO NOT WANT THIS POWER OF ATTORNEY TO CONTINUE IF YOU BECOME INCAPACITATED.

EXERCISE OF POWER OF ATTORNEY WHERE MORE THAN ONE AGENT DESIGNATED

If I have designated more than one agent, the agents are to act

_____

IF YOU APPOINTED MORE THAN ONE AGENT AND YOU WANT EACH AGENT TO BE ABLE TO ACT ALONE WITHOUT THE OTHER AGENTS JOINING, WRITE THE WORD "SEPARATELY" IN THE BLANK SPACE ABOVE. IF YOU DO NOT INSERT ANY WORD IN THE BLANK SPACE, OR IF YOU INSERT THE WORD "JOINTLY," THEN ALL OF YOUR AGENTS MUST ACT OR SIGN TOGETHER.

I agree that any third party who receives a copy of this document may act under it. Revocation of the power of attorney is not effective as to a third party until the third party has actual knowledge of the revocation. I agree to indemnify the third party for any claims that arise against the third party because of reliance on this power of attorney.

Signed this _____ day of _____, 199___.

_____

Social Security Number:

_____

State of California
County of _____

On _____, 199___, before me, [notary], personally appeared _____, personally known to me to be the person whose name is subscribed to the within instrument and acknowledged to me that he/she/they executed the same in his/her/their authorized capacity(ies), and that by his/her/their signature(s) on the instrument the person(s), or the entity upon behalf of which the person(s) acted, executed the instrument.

WITNESS my hand and official seal. _____

BY ACCEPTING OR ACTING UNDER THE APPOINTMENT, THE AGENT ASSUMES THE FIDUCIARY AND OTHER LEGAL RESPONSIBILITIES OF AN AGENT.

COMMUNITY PROPERTY AFFIDAVIT

We, [HUSBAND] and [WIFE], husband and wife, hereby declare that all of the property that we hold in our names as joint tenants or tenants in common or property in a living trust of which we are the Settlors formerly held by us in joint tenancy or as tenants in common is our community property with the exception of any bank or savings account standing in our names as joint tenants.

EXECUTED this ____ day of _____, 199___, at _____, California.

_____   _____
HUSBAND   WIFE

NOMINATION OF CONSERVATOR

I, _____, hereby nominate the following individuals, in the order in which they are named, as the conservator or my person:

[First nominee]

[Second nominee]

I, _____, hereby nominate the following individuals, in the order in which they are named, as the conservator or my estate:

[First nominee]

[Second nominee]

In the event the first nominee fails to qualify or ceases to act as my conservator, I nominate the second nominee as conservator to act in his or her stead.

No bond shall be required of any of the above-nominated conservators.

This Nomination of Conservator hereby revokes all prior nominations.

Dated: _____   _____

[Declarant]

CONFIDENTIAL CLIENT QUESTIONNAIRE

(ASSET INFORMATION)

NAME _____ SPOUSE'S NAME: _____

ESTIMATED VALUE OF GROSS ESTATE: _____

ASSETS

A. Real Property

For each parcel of real property owned by you, please attach a copy of the deed and provide the following information:

Address:_____

How Title Held: _____

Estimated Fair Market Value: _____

Present Encumbrance: _____

Name of Lender(s): _____

(Please attach additional sheets if you own more than one parcel of real property).

B. Corporate Securities

[If your securities are held in a brokerage account, you may simply attach a copy of a recent statement.

Name of Security   Value

_____ $ _____

_____ $ _____

_____ $ _____

How Title Held: _____

Location of Certificates: _____

Name and Address of Stock Broker:_____

C. Cash

Bank Account/Location	*How Held	Approx. Balance
_____	_____	$ _____
_____	_____	$ _____
_____	_____	$ _____
_____	_____	$ _____
_____	_____	$ _____
_____	_____	$ _____
_____	_____	$ _____

*How Bank Accounts Held (i.e. joint tenancy, individually, tenants in common)

D. Life Insurance

For each life insurance policy owned, please provide the following:

Company/Policy No.	Face Value	Beneficiary(ies)	Owner(s)
_____	$ _____	_____	_____
_____	$ _____	_____	_____
_____	$ _____	_____	_____
_____	$ _____	_____	_____

E. Personal Property

Please state the approximate value of all tangible personal property owned by you and its location:

_____

Among your tangible personal property, are there any antiques or objects of art? [Yes/No] If yes, please state estimated value.

F. Retirement/Pension Plans

For each retirement, pension, or profitsharing plan, please state the following:

Employer: _____

Type of Plan: _____

Designated Beneficiary(ies): _____

_____

_____

Name and Address of Plan Administrator: _____

_____

_____

G. Client-owned Business

Name: _____ Type: _____

Other owners: _____

Is there a buy-sell agreement? _____

H. Partnership Interests

Name of Partnership: _____

Name(s) of Other Partner(s): _____

I. Unsecured Liabilities (over $2,500)

Amount Owed   Payee

$ _____   _____

$ _____   _____

J. Other Assets [i.e., interest in lawsuit, copyrights, patents, mineral rights]

_____

_____

_____

K. Safe Deposit Box: _____ Location: _____

   Location of Key: _____

L. Accountant

   Name and address of your accountant and/or tax adviser:

   _____

   _____

   _____

M. Do you have a beneficial interest in a trust? If so, please provide a copy of the trust.

N. Do you expect to inherit property in the foreseeable future? If so, please describe what you expect to inherit and from whom.

O. Have you made gifts of over $10,000 to anyone? If yes, please provide the name of the person, the date of the gift, and the value of the gift.

   Did you file gift tax returns?

P. Please indicate any special burial or funeral instructions you wish your Executor to know about.

CONFIDENTIAL CLIENT QUESTIONNAIRE
(FAMILY INFORMATION)

DATE: _____

NAME: _____   SPOUSE'S NAME: _____

HOME ADDRESS: _____

_____

Home Telephone Number: _____ Work: _____.

Your Birthdate: _____ Spouse's Birthdate: _____

Your Social Security number: _____

Spouse's Social Security number: _____

Both spouses U. S. citizens? _____ If not, please indicate citizenship:

NAME(S) OF CHILD(REN):
(Include birthdates, marital status, telephone numbers, and addresses)

NAME(S) OF CHILD(REN) OF SPOUSE:
(Include birthdates, marital status, telephone numbers, and addresses)

NAME(S) OF GRANDCHILD(REN) OF EACH SPOUSE:
(Include birthdates and addresses, and identify parent)

NAMES OF YOUR PARENTS, IF LIVING: _____

NAMES OF YOUR SPOUSE'S PARENTS, IF LIVING: _____

If you have neither living parents nor children, please give the name, relationship, and address of your next of kin and of your spouse's next of kin:

CHECKLIST OF THINGS TO DISCUSS WITH YOUR OWN CLEVER ATTORNEY

1. Should you have a will or a living trust?

2. If you are married, do you need:

    (A) A tax savings trust (bypass trust)? (Probably, if the estate of you and your spouse is likely to exceed $600,000.)

    (B) A QTIP trust? (Probably, if you want to control what happens to your property after both you and your spouse are gone.)

    (C) A special power of appointment? (Probably, if you want to give your spouse the ability to control what happens to your property after your death.)

    (D) A QDOT trust? (Probably, if either of you is not a U.S. citizen and either of you has assets worth over $600,000.)

    (E) A community property affidavit? (Probably, if you live in a community property state and own appreciated property.)

    (F) A durable general power of attorney? (Probably, if you have a living trust or want an inexpensive alternative to a conservatorship in the event of a temporary disability.)

3. If you have children:

    (A) How do you want to leave bequests to minor children?

    　　(1) To a guardian?

    　　(2) To a trustee?

    　　(3) To a custodian under the California Uniform Transfers to Minors Act?

    (B) Do you want to make annual exclusion gifts to your children? If so, how do you want to leave the gifts?

    　　(1) To a Custodian under the California Uniform Transfers to Minors Act?

    　　(2) To a minor's trust?

    　　(3) To a Crummey trust?

    (C) Should you establish a qualified personal residence trust? (Possibly, if you don't mind a bit of a gamble.)

4. If you have grandchildren, do you want to create a generation-skipping trust? (Probably, if you are interested in saving your grandchildren taxes.)

5. Should you execute the following documents:

    (A) A durable power of attorney for health care? (Probably, if there is someone to whom you are willing to delegate your health care decisions.)

(B) A living will? (Probably, if there is no one to whom you are willing to delegate your health care decisions and if you don't want your life artificially prolonged.)

(C) A Nomination of Conservator? (Probably, especially if you don't have a living trust.)

6. If you are charitably minded: Should you make gifts of appreciated property to charity? Should you establish, during your life or at death, a charitable remainder trust?

A SIMPLIFIED GLOSSARY OF TERMS

Author's Note: Following are nontechnical, nonwindy definitions of the concepts covered in this book. They are accurate as far as they go. But if you really want full-blown, detailed definitions, you should consult *Black's Law Dictionary* or other more definitive legal texts.

Alternate valuation date for estate tax purposes, the date six months after the date of death upon which assets may be valued.

Annual exclusion up to $10,000 you can give away annually to each of any number of people, tax free.

Basis, tax what you paid for an asset (in the case of real property, less depreciation plus any improvements).

Beneficiary, life insurance the person (or entity) who, upon the death of the insured, is entitled to receive the insurance proceeds.

Beneficiary, trust the person(s) entitled to receive distributions from a trust.

Bond a written undertaking by a bonding company to protect the estate from losses resulting from theft by the trustee, conservator, or guardian.

Bypass trust a trust, containing up to the exemption amount($600,000), that escapes tax in the surviving spouse's estate.

California inheritance tax not to worry, repealed in 1982.

California Uniform Transfers to Minors Act legislation providing a simple, inexpensive way to transfer property to a custodian for the benefit of a minor.

Capital gains tax income tax you pay on the gain (the difference between an asset's basis and its sales price) when you sell an asset.

Certification, legal attestation by the State Bar of California that an attorney has qualified as an expert in a particular field.

Charitable remainder trust a trust, eventually passing to charity, that pays you or your family members a set amount of money each year.

Community property property acquired during your marriage other than by gift or inheritance.

Community property affidavit a document confirming that all property held in the name of you and your spouse is community property.

Conservatee the person for whom a conservatorship is established.

Conservator of the estate the court-appointed person (or entity) having the responsibility for the conservatee's financial affairs.

Conservator of the person the court-appointed person (or entity) having the responsibility for the conservatee's personal care.

Corporation a business entity in which the liability of its shareholders is limited to the value of its assets.

Crummey trust a trust, usually established for the benefit of a child, that is not required to terminate when the child reaches age 21.

Directive to physicians a document directed to your doctor stating that you do not want your life artificially prolonged.

Disclaimer a document in which you give up your right to all or part of an inheritance.

Durable power of attorney for health care a document in which you appoint someone to make health care decisions for you in the event you are unable to do so.

Durable power of attorney, general a document that survives your incompetency and gives another person the right to conduct your financial affairs.

Estate taxes taxes imposed by the federal government at your death based on the value of the property in your estate.

Executor, executrix the person (or entity) appointed by the court to administer your estate.

Exempt assets assets not subject to creditors' claims.

Exemption, federal the value of assets ($600,000) you can give away during life or at death that is not subject to gift or estate tax.

Extraordinary fees additional fees charged by the probate attorney, subject to court approval, for services not covered by the probate fee.

Fiscal year a tax year, as distinguished from a calendar year, that can be chosen for income tax purposes after your death.

Fraudulent conveyance a transfer of assets made primarily for the purpose of avoiding creditors' claims.

General partnership a partnership in which all partners are liable for partnership obligations.

Generation-skipping trust a trust into which you put up to $1,000,000 that will pass to your grandchildren without being taxed in your children's estates.

Gift taxes taxes imposed by the federal government on lifetime transfers.

Gross estate the value of your entire estate undiminished by allowable deductions such as debts or administration expenses.

Guardian of the estate the court-appointed person (or entity) having the responsibility for a minor's financial affairs.

Guardian of the person the court-appointed person (or entity) having the responsibility for a minor's personal care.

Homestead exemption the value of your home protected from creditors' claims.

Insured the person whose death causes insurance proceeds to be payable to a named beneficiary.

Intestate succession the manner in which your estate passes under California law if you die without a will.

Inventory and appraisement the document filed in either a probate, a conservatorship, or a guardianship proceeding that lists and values all assets of the estate.

Investigator, court a county employee, reporting directly to the superior court, who evaluates conservatorships and guardianships.

Joint tenancy a method of holding property in the names of two or more people such that upon the death of one the property passes to the survivor(s).

Limited liability company a business entity that is taxed like a partnership but affords the same protection as a corporation.

Limited partnership a partnership in which the liability of the limited partners is restricted to their investment in the company.

Limited power of appointment the power to direct to whom assets will ultimately pass within a limited class of beneficiaries.

Living trust a trust established primarily for the purpose of avoiding probate that is also used as a substitute for a conservatorship.

Marital deduction, unlimited a deduction for federal gift and estate tax purposes that allows you to make unlimited gifts to your spouse tax free.

Marketability discount a discount in value attributable to an asset's being subject to a buyout agreement.

Martindale-Hubbell Law Directory a periodical that provides information on attorneys.

Medi-Cal a combined state and federal program providing nursing home benefits.

Medicare a federal program, run as a part of the Social Security system, providing medical benefits.

Minority discount a discount in value attributable to an asset's not being a controlling interest.

Minor's trust a trust, established for the benefit of a child, that terminates when the child reaches age 21.

Nomination of conservator a document in which you nominate your conservator and, if you choose, waive any bond requirement.

Offshore trust a trust established in a foreign country for the purpose of avoiding creditors' claims.

Pick-up tax a portion of your federal estate tax payable to the state of California.

Principal, trust the body of a trust that usually bears interest.

Probate the legal process for the orderly distribution of your estate.

Probate fee the fee, established by law, to which your estate representative and the probate attorney are entitled.

QDOT trust (qualified domestic trust) a trust for the benefit of a noncitizen spouse that qualifies for the unlimited marital deduction.

QPRT trust (qualified personal residence trust) a trust into which the grantor transfers his or her residence, reserving an interest for a stated number of years, with the remainder passing usually to his or her children.

QTIP trust (qualified terminable interest property trust) a trust for the benefit of your spouse that qualifies for the unlimited marital deduction.

Special needs trust a trust for a disabled person, intended to supplement rather than replace public benefit payments.

Spendthrift provision a trust provision that protects a beneficiary's interest in a trust from creditors' claims.

Sprinkling power the power of a trustee to make discretionary distributions to a class of beneficiaries you designate.

Statute of Elizabeth the first statute declaring transfers in fraud of creditors to be void.

Taxable estate your gross estate less deductions such as debts and administration expenses.

Ward a minor for whom a guardianship has been established.

Will a document stating how your property will be disposed of upon your death.

Are my utilities (IRA & non) in my estate, or commun. prop.?
What changes if we execute a commun prop affidavit?
Should E. give me 230.5 to balance accts, or put in trust?